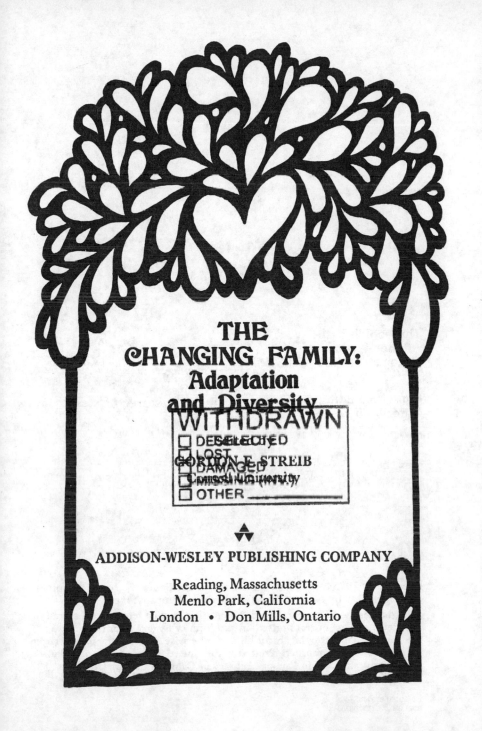

THE
CHANGING FAMILY:
Adaptation
and Diversity

GORDON F. STREIB
Cornell University

ADDISON-WESLEY PUBLISHING COMPANY

Reading, Massachusetts
Menlo Park, California
London • Don Mills, Ontario

This book is in the
Addison-Wesley Series in
Dialogues in the Social Sciences

Consulting Editor
Marcello Truzzi

ISBN 0-201-07320-X
CDEFGHIJKL-DO-7987654

Contents

III.
Case Studies of Diversity and Adaptation

IV.
Forecasting the Future of the Family
Continuity and Diversity

Introduction

Some of the basic assumptions and practices of Western society that were formerly taken for granted are now being questioned sharply. Indeed some critics are not interested in mere verbal criticism; they wish to destroy the old order and rebuild a new form of society. Traditional family values and practices are especially singled out for attack.

On all sides we hear statements that the family as presently constituted is obsolete, and that society must find new forms and patterns if the family is to survive. We also hear that men and women are not happy in their personal relationships in marriage; that women are prevented from reaching their true human potential by traditional family arrangements; that children are not being reared to be "whole people"; that partners are increasingly finding sexual satisfaction outside of marriage. Some critics maintain that marriage and family life patterns are so pernicious that *any* change in family patterns will be an improvement. For example, in a recent book, *The Death of the Family,* David Cooper presents an impassioned denunciation of the family. He maintains that the family is stultifying and sometimes lethal for its members because families glue people together too much. He also claims that families instill social controls which are too stringent and perpetuate an outmoded and elaborate set of taboos which in reality are chains which prevent one from reaching his true potential.

The women's liberation movement is also critical of traditional family patterns and the prescribed female roles. Some segments

1

of the new left political movement are equally dissatisfied with present family arrangements because they perpetuate bourgeois society and thus are considered to be major impediments to the creation of a more human, communal type of society.

Persons who hold a more traditional view of the political and economic institutions are also concerned with the breakdown of the family and point out that one out of every four marriages ends in divorce. Ignoring the fact that most of these divorcees promptly remarry, these critics say that such statistics are evidence of the "failure of the family."

Certainly there have been many factors that have altered the norms and expectations about marriage and the family in the last century. Most of these influences will undoubtedly persist for many years in the future. Some of the changes, however, may only affect a minority of persons, for the present modal pattern will still probably involve the majority of Americans of the next generation in the traditional ways of organizing family life. For example, most men will continue to fulfill the economic function of the family by being the principal breadwinners; most preschool children will continue to be reared at home, despite the increase in daycare centers; most young couples will still aspire to a legal marriage and a household of their own, in spite of the increasing formation of communes and informal sexual liaisons; most people will continue to turn to their families in times of trouble or crisis, and not to social agencies. Yet, there will be growing acceptance of diverse ways of fulfilling family functions of economic maintenance, emotional support, socialization of children, and sexual expression.

"Family" is a word with many meanings; thus it is essential that we clarify what the term means in the context of this anthology. Sociologists usually distinguish between the family as an institution and the family as a group. The first meaning considers the family as one of the major social structures—like the economy and the polity—and views the family in somewhat abstract, depersonalized form. On the other hand, one may use the word "family" to mean a functioning, face-to-face group that shares a common purpose, interacts, and takes part in several significant activities related to having and rearing children.

Two other concepts whose meaning needs to be clarified are courtship and marriage. These terms are obviously closely related to the family but they are separate and distinct in themselves. One way to demarcate them in relation to the family is to view the family in terms of a process of family formation. The traditional view of these three components of the family system is that the three aspects—courtship, marriage and family—proceed in an orderly and inevitable fashion. In earlier societies, the step-by-step development probably did not always take place, yet this is the norm which was prescribed as "proper behavior."

In contemporary Western societies, like the United States, these traditional and prescribed patterns of courtship, marriage, and family are often no longer seen as "natural" stages leading from one to another. There are some social critics who advocate and practice a lifetime of courtship in which they do not desire a marital union or a family group. They point to the dangers of overpopulation, and maintain that they are being more "moral" than those with conventianal family ideals. This point of view is becoming more widely accepted and it is one form of diversity in the family system. Furthermore, some people now desire marriage but do not desire a family group. They may prefer serial marriages, with a new and intense relationship every few years, and no permanent commitments. The number of adults with families but no spouses is also on the increase; this group consists not only of single-parent families resulting from divorce, death, or desertion, but more unwed mothers are now electing to keep their babies instead of relinquishing them for adoption.

Thus the guidelines of what is considered "proper behavior" are less sharply defined than in the past. Although many people conceive of the family in stereotyped terms, as the "Dick-and-Jane" family of the traditional first-grade reader, we see that there is already great diversity in this country, and growing acceptance of that diversity. While the new forms of marriage and family life are adopted by only a small segment of adults, they receive considerable attention and publicity. The student of the family needs to know what the modal family patterns are and what the forms are that are less frequently observed. The unusual, the bizarre, and the idiosyncratic forms are often highly publicized, and thus assumed to be modalities when, in fact, they are not.

Many people may be attracted by the new forms but do not have the energy or the adventurousness to innovate. This tends to keep many persons in the traditional patterns which entail less risk and social disapproval. The conventional roles have great utility for many persons both because they are familiar, and also because some anticipatory socialization has already taken place to orient them to traditional family roles and responsibilities. Finally, traditional family roles and duties may be socially and psychologically fulfilling for many persons.

This book brings together a series of selections. Section I focuses on some of the major issues involved in the current criticism of the family system. Section II shows the diversity of family structures and relations which are already present in our society. We may generalize in terms of modal patterns: a father who supports his family, and a mother who keeps house and rears the children; yet many other patterns are observed in this country. Section III includes selections which describe some of the diverse forms of marriage and family life which are being practiced or are being advocated. The last selection in Section IV is the attempt of one sociologist to offer a prediction of how present traditional forms may mesh with changing trends and form courtship, marriage, and family patterns in 1990.

There is a need to add a few words about the selection of the articles which comprise the anthology. They were selected with the the primary purpose of stimulating serious discussion and encouraging further insights by students of the family into the possibilities of diverse family forms in a changing society. Some articles are descriptive and others are more factual. Some writers have taken an opinionated and a controversial position on an issue or on the topic they discuss. Others are more sober and attempt to be judicious in presenting their point of view. Therefore the reader is cautioned not to expect equally rigorous sociological description and analysis in all selections.

In conclusion, we wish to consider adaptations of the family structure not as inevitable evolutionary developments, but as possibilities which may become social reality for varying numbers of people. It is increasingly clear that greater tolerance and acceptance of diversity in family structure and organization seem essential in our pluralistic society.

I

Examination
of the Issues

1

What is the Future of Marriage

Judy Nichol
A dialogue between Mrs. Pat Novick-Raby and
Father Francis L. Filas

In this dialogue, a priest and a sociologist present two opposing points of view regarding family relationships. It was chosen because it highlights some of the complexities of the issues involved in analyzing the family and indicates the broad implications for social changes in the family.

Father Filas and Mrs. Novick-Raby start with different assumptions, not only about family relationships but also about human nature in general: Is man basically humane, good, and kind or does he have elements of "barbarism" in his basic make-up? How much diversity can society permit? The traditional point of view claims that too much diversity is dysfunctional for families and for society. The innovators, like Mrs. Novick-Raby, argue that there should be much greater diversity in man-woman relations and that society can tolerate more variety than the traditionalists assert.

The two discussants also differ in their evaluation of what the government's role should be in regard to family formation and subsequent fertility. The traditional and innovative viewpoints indicate the depth of some of the issues related to new family forms, and how adaptation of the family may run counter to deeply held value positions of some groups.   —GFS

Reprinted with permission from Showcase, *Chicago Sun-Times*, August 1, 1971.

MODERATOR: Will each of you give your views on the subject of marriage?

FATHER FILAS: I stand definitely for preserving the traditional viewpoint of marriage. I think there should be an attempt to save most of the marriages that are breaking up. There should be more premarital training on human values. People should think much more before they enter into these unions called marriages.

MRS. NOVICK-RABY: I believe in a diversified society. That is not to say that the traditional marriage is not a valid or good or honorable choice.

But there should be no stigma attached to people who decide on different choices, such as childless marriages, not marrying, or raising children collectively.

In the past, husbands and wives would die and we would have what was called serial monogamy — from one to another. People have always had needs for some kind of change.

Also there is a basic alienation in society. Jobs aren't satisfactory and all one's needs are concentrated in one person, as opposed to a wider range of family — grandparents, aunts, children. In addition a lot more people are marrying.

FATHER FILAS: I think implicit in the question of the divorce rate is an error that assumes that somewhere or other in the past there was a Golden Age where human relationships were practically perfect and led to idealized marriages. From the beginning the traditional values in marriage were ideals. I thoroughly subscribe to the view that all of us have a veneer of "civilization" and underneath we have to be very careful that the barbaric animal, raging to be let loose, is not let loose.

What I mean by the traditional ideal of marriage is one man, one woman, in a closed, permanent relationship oriented to helping each other and the children who would come. By helping children, I mean to receive them into the world, to rear, discipline, train and love them.

MRS. NOVICK-RABY: I don't think people are barbaric. I think my students have integrity and concern for other human beings. I don't think in this situation there is a need for legal binding marriages. Because of ethical and moral commitments I think people will remain loyal to one another.

FATHER FILAS: Why do you discard what you call legalistic codes?

MRS. NOVICK-RABY: I don't think the state should have anything to do in defining or prescribing the relationships between people. Decisions about dissolution of marriage, or relationships, or changing them should be left up to the couple. I believe they would become more moral and ethical.

FATHER FILAS: I appreciate your belief in the goodness of human nature and the individual responsibility of most people. But this has not been the history of the human race. The reason we have the state involved in marriage is that the state considers this necessary for its survival.

I don't want to be forced to defend the absolute inhumanities of the past and the oppression of women perpetuated under the name of the traditional marriage. In various cultures marriage has been used to treat women as property, to interfere with her value as a human being.

The traditional marriage came into existence to help women.

Traditional marriage, properly understood, is there to safeguard the woman's rights, not to let her be simply the plaything of man's passion and to satisfy his power drive, and be considered his property.

To my mind the basic drive in marriage is the power drive, and marriage is a way of controlling this drive.

I don't think the governments of the world would like the idea of giving up their control over marriage and the family.

MRS. NOVICK-RABY: I think it's a changing society and I think the movement away from state control and toward freedom for the individual is an important principle that we should push forward.

Regarding the point that marriage "protects" women, I think that the notion of protection implies inferiority.

In a diversified society, where different kinds of relationships exist, some families might follow the traditional pattern. In other families some men, who are more loving and warm and understanding and able to deal with children, would care for the children. It may be in some families it would be the female who would be employed.

FATHER FILAS: Do you mean that the woman would no longer be in the position of the mother of the children in bringing them up with her affection, training and time?

MRS. NOVICK-RABY: It would depend on the situation. Some men would care for children, and some women would, depending upon who was best at it.

FATHER FILAS: The view that the father should play a part in bringing up the child is in no way excluded in the traditional view of marriage. Sound people in family life (education) have been saying for a quarter of a century that the husband should take part in bringing up the child.

I would say, however, that I don't think he should do this full time, because I still say that a woman has things to contribute that men can never contribute — each sex has its particular gifts.

MRS. NOVICK-RABY: In some situations the male might be the better child-raiser. In some situations it might be more than one adult. In some situations people shouldn't have children. I'm talking about a society where there is no stigma for diversity.

FATHER FILAS: Historically, organized governments and organized churches have discarded the idea of a too-diversified society on the basis that this would put the society out of existence.

Some of your alternatives, whether it's the deliberately childless marriage or the so-called homosexual union (which is no marriage at all, it's a travesty, it's taking the word marriage and warping it, giving it a meaning that marriage doesn't have) would wipe a society out of existence.

I believe that our society will continue only if we follow the traditional view of marriage.

MRS. NOVICK-RABY: I don't think a diversified society would be chaotic or would expire.

FATHER FILAS: I'd like to go back to some historical examples of why marriage evolved.

In the Middle Ages the typical male and female were having promiscuous unions and this meant that the male was using the female, simply any female that came along and he'd use her and then drop her after she'd be pregnant. Then she's left with the children, who have no father. And so in an attempt to stop this dehumanization of the woman and the child the church put in a rule that marriages had to be witnessed.

Back in the Mesopotamian society of 2,000 B. C. men's most valuable possessions were in this order: sons and male slaves, then possessions, animals, money, wives, concubines, and finally female slaves. The female slave in the olden times was practically without value.

The laws of adultery in the olden times made the woman the adultress, never the man who was committing it at the same time.

At least the ideals of today are higher.

MRS. NOVICK-RABY: Women have always had some value because motherhood was necessary to increase our population to have more people to do the work. Now, with the population explosion, there will not be the same emphasis on motherhood.

FATHER FILAS: I think the population explosion is a misnomer. I don't think the state has any right to control the number of children a family has, that's the essence of freedom.

MRS. NOVICK-RABY: I don't think the state has the right to determine what kind of relationships people have either.

MODERATOR: Father Filas, do you define marriage as a permanent relationship set up to receive children?

FATHER FILAS: It's a closed relationship (that's very essential so we don't have polygamous relationships) and it's to last. It is oriented to bring new life into the world, but not just that. You don't just bring a child into the world and forget about it.

 If it's not permanent the couple will not be sufficiently motivated to overcome the difficulties that meet them in life together.

MODERATOR: With all the difficulties you mention in the beginning would you favor some kind of a trial marriage?

FATHER FILAS: No. The engagement is the time when the values of the so-called trial marriage would be discovered.

MODERATOR: Do you think it is possible for a couple to know enough about each other to make a permanent commitment without sleeping together?

FATHER FILAS: The sex that is tried outside of marriage is overwhelmingly not the sex that is experienced in marriage, simply because the personality relationship is so utterly different in a closed marriage than in the passing courtship.

 There is no such thing as premarital sex. There's merely non-marital sex. Purposefulness for genital sexuality exists only within the marital state.

MRS. NOVICK-RABY: I don't think people should get or remain married because it's good for their character, but because there is some kind of joy and happiness in their relationship.

 Premarital sex and trial marriages are happening. Many of my students make this choice, and I think they make it in a very serious way. Ten years ago male students talked about what they could "get." Now I think people are looking for options for new human relationships and their sexuality is not the reason for trial marriages.

FATHER FILAS: I have been before groups where the girls will give me anonymous written questions saying, 'Why does the girl always suffer?' This is where the girl has to harden herself. I've talked at homes for unwed mothers where the girls are so bitter because when they got pregnant the boy said 'That's your business.' The girl is left standing while the boy gets another partner.

It's not just in pregnancy that the girl always gets hurt. The female is utterly different from the male. The female is involved temperamentally as the male never can get involved. There are many more female suicides over broken love affairs than male suicides. Jokingly, it's been said that the male is miserable after a broken love affair until he gets his next meal.

MRS. NOVICK-RABY: I also think the male suffers. Both sexes are caught in rigid definitions of how they're supposed to behave. So the guys feel a need to be superjock and to lie about their sexuality and their feelings — not because of male temperament, but because of the expectations of society about what is manly.

MODERATOR: Mrs. Novick-Raby, if you believe the state shouldn't have anything to do with marriage, why did you get married?

MRS. NOVICK-RABY: When you are part of a social movement you choose the places where you wish to struggle. On this issue we felt we really didn't have any choice. It was an accommodation to society. I met a great man and we fell in love and that was the only choice available to us.

2

Revolution
in Sex Behavior

Pitirim A. Sorokin

The idea that marriage is the "culminating point of human existence," is expressed by Pitirim A. Sorokin, one of the world's most distinguished sociological scholars.

He argues from an evolutionary and adaptive point of view that traditional marriage and sex relations are essential for the survival and well-being of societies. This selection is presented in juxtaposition to a number of others which are highly critical of conventional prescribed norms for marriage and the family. —GFS

* * *

Birth, marriage, and death are the great events in the life of any individual, for they mark the beginning, middle, and end of each human existence. All societies have viewed them as of the utmost importance, not only for the individual, but also for the survival and well-being of the community. Thus every society has most carefully defined and regulated the customs concerning these events. And of them, marriage has been considered as important, and has been as carefully regulated, as have the mores relating to birth and death.

The reasons for this high evaluation of marriage are obvious. Marriage is a social evidence of the physical, mental, emotional, spiritual, and civic maturity of the individual. It involves the mo-

Reprinted with permission from Pitirim A. Sorokin, *The American Sex Revolution*, Porter Sargent Publisher, Extending Horizons Books, 1956.

mentous transformation of a boy into a husband-father, and of a girl into a wife-mother, with corresponding changes in their social position, privileges, and responsibilities. For a large majority of men and women, marriage is the most vital, the most intimate, and the most complete unification of body, mind, and spirit into one socially approved, indivisible "we". In a good marriage, the individual egos of the parties merge. The joys and sorrows of one become the joys and sorrows of the other. All their values, aspirations, and life-experiences become fully shared. Their mutual loyalty is unconditionally pledged until death do part them. The bond of marriage is truly sacred and indissoluble.

Such an all-embracing union serves as the most powerful antidote against loneliness. It develops and expresses love at its noblest and best, in the moral ennoblement of the married and the true socialization of their children.

From the remotest past, married parents have been the most effective teachers of their children, and the family has been the most important school for the transformation of newly-born human animals into intelligent, socially responsible personalities. This decisive educational role is well summed up in the dictum: "What the family is, such will the society be."

Furthermore, the cultivation of mutual love and the task of educating their children stimulate married persons to release and develop their best creative impulses. For surely the mission of molding their own and their children's personalities is as ennobling as the creation of a masterpiece in the arts or sciences. And regardless of education, social status, religion, or economic conditions, each married couple derives from a good marriage the fullest satisfaction of this creative urge which is in all of us. In this sense, marriage is the most universal and the most democratic school for the development of the creative potential of every human being. This creative urge is possibly the most distinctive mark of the human species, and its satisfaction is an absolute necessity for human happiness.

Enjoying the marital union in its infinite richness, parents freely fulfill many other paramount tasks. They maintain the procreation of the human race. Through their progeny they determine the hereditary and acquired characteristics of future generations. Through marriage they achive a social immortality of their own, of their ancestors, and of their particular groups and community. This immortality is secured through the transmission of their name and values, and of their traditions and ways of life to their children, grandchildren, and later generations.

The fulfillment of these tasks explains why marriage has been regarded by all societies as the culminating point of human existence, and as the most decisive factor in the survival and well-being of the societies themselves.

In contrast to marriage, illicit sex relations cannot and do not fulfill these tasks. The relations between a prostitute and her client, between a mistress and her patron, and between all sorts of incidental "lovers", have never been considered as evidence of mental, moral, or social maturity of the partners. On the contrary, they have been viewed as a sin, or as a crime, or as a symptom of moral and social degeneration of the partners involved. Usually, illicit sex relations rarely go beyond a shortlived "copulational" union. Each partner remains a mere sex apparatus for the satisfaction of the lust of the other. The partners remain largely unknown to each other; their egos are not merged into one "we" nor is their selfishness tempered by mutual devotion and love.

3

The Family
is Out of Fashion

Ann Richardson Roiphe

Is the family really outmoded as some modern critics have charged? Ann Richardson Roiphe relates her analysis to the personal situation in her own immediate family and in her kin network. She points out how some persons romanticize the large, extended family of bygone years, and even dream of reconstituting it. But the reintigration of the extended family is very difficult if not impossible not only because of the geographic dispersal of the members but because it would require the abrogation of basic cultural developments — personal self-realization, free choice of mate and of career — which have required a long time to build into the social structure. Mrs. Roiphe also makes very explicit a fact that many writers leave unsaid, namely, that both critics and defenders of the traditional family presumably have the *same end* in mind, "a society in which each man can live creatively and experience self-love and love of others."
—GFS

"Blood is thicker than water only in the sense of being the vitalizing stream of a certain social stupidity."

David Cooper, *The Death of the Family*

In a silent room on West 79th Street in New York City, 10 women rub their hands rhythmically over their large, pregnant bellies while their husbands stare at stop watches, encouragingly giving hand signals. The couples are in training for natural childbirth with Mrs. Elizabeth Bing, who has spread the gospel in this country that male and female should share in the dramatic event of the birth of their child. Fifty to sixty new couples sign up for this course a month. What are they all doing? What are they doing several months later, walking around in their nursing bras, buying mobiles that swing from crib tops and potties with musical boxes and on and on into a future radically different from that of their childless past? Don't they know, this army of young people pushing strollers through the park, that they are behaving in a reactionary way? The nuclear family is not now a thing of fashion.

Weary from long discussions on economic theory and wasted by years of futile peace marches, bored by campaigns for compromise candidates and stunned by pollution and ecology reports, the intellectual community has turned with primal fury against a newly discovered evil: the family. Women's Liberation points out again and again how burdened, minimal and trivial is the life of the woman who tends the family. Books are appearing that attack the nuclear unit as the source of the alienated, bomb-throwing society we have come to know all too well. The call is out for new structures, babies brought up in day-care centers, new communes—or perhaps, as Germaine Greer proposes, let us do away with connected permanent relationships entirely. Let each man, woman and child shift for himself. Like the insects that fly singly throughout the ephemeral summer days.

One night my teen-aged stepdaughter tearfully accused her father of being interested in her only if she was accepted into a good college so he could enjoy a little reflected status. My God, I thought, she's talking about the man who burped her, carried her to the zoo, played endless games of Monopoly and Clue, and stood in 100-degree heat to watch her ride dumb beasts in meaningless circles around a dusty ring. She's talking about the man who carried 10 bottles of ketchup all through Europe because she wouldn't eat anything without it. How did she miss the tenderness, despair, passion, pride and fear he feels for her? Of course,

I knew the facts. She has to grow away, to tear apart the first love and start again—but how painful the ripping of the sinews, how wretched we all become in the process.

I looked at our new baby. "Da, da," she says with joy, pulling off her father's glasses. He kisses her on the stomach. She laughs, cosmic, total, beautiful pleasure—but where is it going? Is it worth it? Sometimes it seems as if the tensions, the angers we have accumulated against each other will get together and flood out this family, each of us floating apart on a river of nightmares, to drown eventually.

The other day I looked at my 10-year-old. "Fix your hair," I said, "wash your face. You look like an orphan. Why won't you wear any of the dresses that hang neglected, wasted, in the closet?" Then I listened. It wasn't my voice speaking at all. It was my dead mother, out of my own body, screeching from the grave the very words I had so loathed. Within me the ghost of values past was possessing, displacing the present. Family of origin, family of procreation, tied together, despite my heroic efforts to separate them, to create a pure and different life. Patterns of the past, rejected or accepted, have a way of imposing themselves on the present. We all live with the dark designs of our early loves; our hates and our attractions are colored by the intense experience of family life. We cannot easily be freed. It is true as David Cooper in "The Death of the Family" says, "A thousand ghosts roam within us." They depersonalize, limit and bind us. We are like natives with large disks protruding from distorted lips or like primitive tribes with earlobes stretched to elephantine proportions.

Most people suffer from anxieties, are neurosis-riddled, limited, uncreative, socially normal, but inwardly cut off from feelings of self. That is the usual result of our family system. No one I have ever known has made it through without scars on the psyche that became open wounds on the backs of the next generation and yet I feel as I struggle over the bikes, sled and carriage that block access to our stairway that I and my contemporaries, male and female, are truly engaged in a revolutionary drama. We who live in families are the frontiersmen of a new world. That this was equally true of the generation before, and will apply to the generation after, is not discouraging but from a certain distance merely the stuff of history.

Margaret Mead in writing a text to a photography book on the family, has said that "no society anywhere has ever sanctioned illegitimacy." This means that every society from aborigine to

Maoist China has structured some form of family life to raise, socialize, protect the children—to guarantee instutionally the social,
sexual needs of the adults. Some of these systems have worked
better than others, all of them have demanded a price from the participants—some personal freedoms and instinctual pleasures must be
abandoned when human groups are formed and it is these very restrictions that enemies of the family are now calling abominations.

Germaine Greer would have us set no limit on sexual pleasure,
submit to no discipline of nursing schedules or possessive needs.
She would have us abandon ugly security for free flight. David
Cooper and R. D. Laing incriminate the family unit as the origina-
tor of all pathology, personal and political. They envision a utopia
of people truly separate from one another, each self-realized and
alive in his own present. David Cooper suggests that mothers
should learn not to pick up babies when they wail in the first year
of life, but allow them to experience the desolation and aloneness
of their position. If we do this he promises we will create people
who are not tied to others, not destroyed by the family romance.

His method seems extreme but the goals are unarguable. We
all want better human beings. We want to create a society in which
each man can live creatively and experience self-love and love of
others. We want fewer divorces, fewer psychotics, no Lee Harvey
Oswalds, and finally, in a wonderful new world, no Lyndon Johnsons, no George Wallaces, no bigots, no liars, no destroyers—the
Pentagon turned into a botanical garden. But the question is,
how do we make better people, how will we perfect, tame, simultaneously harness and free the conflicting forces of aggression and
love that are an absolute part of every human child that opens its
new eyes on the jaded world of its parents?

I cannot believe that further disconnection of child from parent, an atomization of each human unit into a single orbiting star
will achieve anything more than the certain death of the species. It
seems self-evident that we are now stuck with one another, parent
and child, male and female, and that the changes that must be made
need to take into account the necessary balances we have to find in
order to assure the separate dignity of each living soul. It is my
baby's right to take her first steps away from me and my obligation to follow, not too close but not too far, for the next moment
when she needs to be restrained from pulling the boiling soup down
on her head.

As my husband and I go about our day, we are trying to form
between us the shape of a family that will enable our children
better to integrate the pressures on them from without and with-

in, and to make them freer, their ghosts more benign than ours, their limitations less paralyzing. We try not to let our time go dead with security and wooden with known experiences. We attempt to do better than our parents—some days we succeed. Very often we definitely don't.

There are alternatives to the nuclear family. I think about them on bad days, when croup has kept us up all night, I've gotten a call about a child turning into a wild thing at school, and some disappointment has turned up in my own work; all combine in a depression, a fatigue common to the battles of family living. First, I romanticize the extended family. Why don't I have a loving aunt to walk the baby, a wise uncle to cover the math homework, a niece to do the shopping and a mother to organize the whole of my day? Why am I so alone in my house without the blood ties, the relatives who would connect me firmly into their tribe and end my recurrent nightmare of standing alone on the edge of a cliff that turns into talcum powder wherever I put my foot?

I imagine myself in a compound in Africa. I see myself as a little girl secure in the bosom of my large family and all the goats they commonly own. I think of myself as a woman pounding grain beside my sisters-in-law. I think of myself as an older woman carrying my daughter's baby in my arms, singing an age-old chant. I compare that image to the image of myself as the unwanted old lady I may live long enough to be, sending expensive presents to distant places, hoping against hope to be invited somewhere for the holidays.

Why not? We could gather five or six cooperative apartments, break through the floors, build interior staircases. The eldest could have the final say in matters of marriage, finance, careers and summer vacations. We could have a large common kitchen, a playroom, bedrooms and office space for the several professionals in my family.

The more specifically I consider this solution, the more I must face certain horrible truths. I would rather live in a swamp of stinging mosquitoes and biting crocodiles than spend a month with my very own blood ties. Because of educational differences, because of major value disagreements, because of the peculiar American experience that allows us to develop, peas from the same pod, into a multitude of fruits and vegetables so different from one another they can no longer cling to the same vine.

We could no longer live together. We speak as many languages as destroyed the Tower of Babel. I have an aunt who wins rumba contests at Grossinger's and another whose daughter was presented

at a debutante cotillion. I have a bigoted uncle and children at the
United Nations School. I have a religious, orthodox father-in-law
and an avant-garde cousin who paints blue lines on mountain
ridges. It is no longer possible for us to reintegrate into an ex-
tended-family unit without violating the development of personality, of free choice, of education, of varied cultural growth that
was so dearly won, so bitterly fought for by several generations of
uneasy Americans.

Is our specialness worth the pains we suffer in not belonging
to a homogeneous, easy-to-understand, easy-to-connect-with culture? In a unified society there would be fewer private disasters,
kids lost in a drug haze, others mouthing Zen prayers in hope of
mystic union when we give them only personal responsibility and
individual terror. There might not be the internal deadness that
the search for security inflicts on seekers after better lawn mowers
and swifter crabgrass killers, but there would also not be radicals,
poets, painters, surgeons, merchants, technocrats or newspapermen.
We would all be herding goats, or nut gathering or hunting fierce
beasts. Today we have no choice—we cannot live in extended-
family units and move in any direction except backwards, where,
despite the comfort offered, most of us are unwilling to go.

But then there is the other much-discussed alternative to the
nuclear-family problem and that is the commune. The family then
becomes a chosen one, of friends who share cultural, social, political outlook, and the society within the commune can be as homogeneous as that of any Samoan island anchored peaceably in the
Pacific. Children could know many relationships and grow up in a
microcosmic world in which they could trust themselves and others.

This prospect has always interested me and I have often
thought about it, flirting with the possibility of emigrating to Israel, to the hills of California or the farms of Pennsylvania—where-
ever a congenial group might be. I have in fact never moved a
muscle to make this a reality and I have finally had to ask myself
why. I think it has to do with the task of personal relationship.
If it is hard for me to manage with honesty, spontaneity and pleasure the limited number of people with whom I am now living—
how ever will I be with many others? Diluting love experiences
will not necessarily enrich them. If I care for 10 with the passion
I now care for one, I will be less to everyone, or so it seems.

I wonder why so many communes break apart. They are
forming and reforming, blasting and changing with such rapidity
that a scientist I knew, attempting to do research on the communal experience, found that as soon as his sources gave him the lo-

cation of a commune, the chances were 50 to 1 that commune would already have been a thing of the past. It seems others besides me would and do have difficulty in group living.

We are a greedy, murderous, cannibalistic and sexually excitable species. This is clear to anyone who has ever taken care of a 2-year-old over an extended period of time. We were thrown out of the Garden of Eden because of our imperfections. It may be that the same humanity which later led Cain to smash in the head of Abel makes commune living problematic. I am not ready to say it is impossible and I would think that there will be movement toward greater community in the near future. As women tend to go out and work, they will need at least partial dependence on one another; as men move to take over some of the burden of domesticity, they may also turn to closer associations with one another. It may be that voluntary groupings, associations of friends, will emerge as a solution to many of the burdens now crushing the nuclear unit.

This will take time to effect and it will take strong, undestroyed people to pioneer in new relationship styles and make them work. Not our weakest, youngest, drug-addled population, but our finest products of education and personal strength will have to venture into new forms of family living if a real social change is to take place. If we are to create more viable forms of family and political life, we need people who can be loving without being inhibited. People who are sufficiently self-controlled so all their emotions don't run amuck, but not so controlled that they don't function creatively in relation to whatever task is set before them. This may be our children, or our grandchildren, or even many generations still to come. The more we learn about how a child grows, the more our schools improve, the more our homes and schools adopt the principles of empathy and love, the closer we will come to positive change.

The communes of America are now isolated from the political and social mainstream of the culture and this also makes it hard to join them and hard for them to sustain themselves. In Israel the commune is a part of the political system, serving both the defense and cultivation of the country. Its members are nourished by their ideological relationship to the rest of the nation. This tells us that the way any family lives is indeed a political event. If in America we cannot employ the commune properly, we can still contribute to the future of our country through the kind of people we are and the kind of children we raise. I am not suggesting family life as the only form of political agitation, only that it is one of the available tools.

The current attacks on the nuclear-family structure must not turn our attention away from the need for better child care, more love, not less, from men and women fully exploring the possibilities of love between themselves. If only the potential of male and female is deemed worthy of concern, we will throw away the real revolution that is in the making: that is, changing society by changing the potential of individual citizens. Each single child now in its stroller, pulling and pushing on the beads that hang before it, sucking at its fingers, mouthing its pacifier, stroking a bit of blanket or ragged toy—each of those babies may grow to be a radically new generation that will make miracles or little steps towards miracles.

It is probably true that revolutions so far have all been corrupted by the tyranny that possesses men when they gain power. It would seem that all the isms of the political spectrum are subject to the same malfunctions of the individuals who live within them. But perhaps a revolution will one day succeed when the children who lead it are less damaged by what has come before.

This is what I am doing, running around to nursery schools, looking at the animals in the zoo, waiting for hours in an Indian Walk shoe store to buy a pair of baby sandals. I have a child afraid of the wind and even a slight breeze sends her rushing for cover. I have another who remains convinced the dark is populated with evil spirits that grind little girls into phosphates, the better to pollute our oceans with. I can't seem to make anyone totally happy or well but the battle is nevertheless joined. I won't do worse than was done before.

The Women's Liberation attack on the nuclear family has made several valid points. Women must have more in their lives than children and homemaking. If they don't, they wait like a lit hand grenade sitting on the diningroom table. In due time, the family is certain to blow up. They have also correctly emphasized freedom of choice for women. Marriage is not to everyone's liking and no modern society, groping for new and better ways, should coerce or ostracize, call sick or anti-social, people whose sexual choices or life styles differ. But the Liberationists' de-emphasis on child care, child development, male and female love, is equally destructive. Women can work, men can share the responsibility for the home, without the family dissolving and without our losing sight of the primary human connections: man, woman and child, each important, not one neglected for the other. These days I feel a cultural pressure not to be absorbed in my child. Am I a Mrs. Portnoy sitting on the head of her little Alex? I am made to feel my curiosity about the growth of my babies is somehow counter-revolutionary. The new tolerance should ultimately respect the lady who wants to make pies as well as the one who majors in higher mathematics.

Now the ecology problem looms. An anthropologist friend of mine pointed out that the antifamily feelings, the rise in active homosexual organizations and the Women's Liberation Front itself are all part of a cultural, collective, unconscious move on the part of the species to save itself from the certain ruin of over-population. I have a hard time imagining or visualizing the collective unconscious at work, but then I have a hard time believing in molecules dancing around in the floor beneath my feet. It seems plausible that the turn against the idealization of family life is a form of population control. I also agree there should be room on the earth but I'm still interested in the quality of the life we are preserving. A nation of Jill Johnsons, a universe of gay bars, a world of men and women staring each other down across the barricades, seems bleak. I cannot imagine a decent library without "Babar," "Winnie-the-Pooh," "The Secret Garden," "The Wizard of Oz," etc.

The women in Mrs. Bing's apartment, practicing their breathing techniques, the ladies waiting in pediatricians' offices, the men who ride their babies on the back of their bikes around the park, who buy tickets at the carrousel, who wipe Italian ices from small chins stained like the rainbow in the sky, have confronted and daily do confront the drama of fate, of love, of age, of biology. Tenderness and fury we all know, failure, fear and envy of our friends' greater successes we all have experienced. Our mettle is tested and we are often found wanting. We face our past each day. We are humiliated by our absurd ambitions. We observe our petty and great sins magnified or modified in our children—but, brothers and sisters, nuclear-family people, for better or worse, the future is ours.

4

Marriage
and the Nuclear Family
as Target

Jessie Bernard

Why is the nuclear family one of the major targets of the contemporary women's liberation movement? Dr. Jessie Bernard, a distinguished sociologist, analyzes the charges that the nuclear family "is the primary agent of sexual repression in this society," and that it has deprived women of their humanity. She points out that the reproductive function (child bearing) must be clearly separated from the socialization function (child rearing). It is obvious that men cannot do the first, but they can participate more fully in the latter. The advocates of social change maintain that the major reorganization of the family requires a shifting of some of the aspects of child-rearing from women to men. Family roles and activities related to socialization in the home must be restructured with men doing much more than they have done traditionally. Another alternative is the provision of more child-rearing agencies outside the family (day care centers, nursery schools, etc.).   —GFS

Reprinted from Jessie Bernard, *Woman and the Public Interest* (Chicago: Aldine • Atherton, Inc., 1971), copyright © 1971 by Jessie Bernard. Reprinted by permission of the author and Aldine • Atherton, Inc.

Related to both sexism and the privatized nuclear family as a target of Movement Women is marriage as now institutionalized. We noted earlier that although marriage had a marked effect on work motivation among women, it had little effect on actual professional achievement. Once committed to a career, the married women showed achievement equal to that of unmarried women. So long as children were not involved, then, marriage as related to the careers of women has little relevance for the public interest. But it still has relevance for Movement Women concerned with self-actualization, not so much because of any effect it might have on careers as because of what sexism in marriage does to the personalities of women.

Although there is a formidable research basis for the charge that marriage as now structured in our society is not good for wives (Bernard, 1971), Movement Women do not rely on this research in their indictments. They rely on their own experiences and observations.

Movement Women feel that women have, in effect, been sold a bill of goods in marriage. Though it "is made to seem attractive and inevitable," marriage "is a trap." They have been programmed from childhood to think that not marrying is a fate worse than death: "Better dead than unwed." They are encouraged to put all their eggs in this one basket. It is their self-fulfillment. Actually it imposes subservience on women and ultimately deprives them of any identity of their own.

The attacks on marriage in the earlier polemics were part of the disillusionment the women experienced in the movement; it was a counterpart of the disillusionment they were experiencing at their exclusion from policy and leadership positions, and it reflected the same male chauvinism. "As [Movement Women] got married, they found that there were no models for a marriage in which both man and woman were politically active. Was the once-active woman now to assume a supportive role, stay home with the kids or get an unwanted job to support her activist husband? Were both partners' interests to have equal weight in determining what kind of work they would do, where they would live?" The answer to the first brace of questions was, apparently, "Yes" to both; to the second, "No, neither."

The picture of the marriages of women in the movement looks grim as depicted in the early polemics. The women "earn the money in the mundane jobs that our society pays people to do, so the radical men can be at home and be political and creative. . . . But in order to do this, these men need followers and maintainers. Thus, the workers of the movement . . . are the typists, fund-raisers and community organizers." One is reminded of the *shtetl* wife, except that she was more than happy to support her learned husband in his studies. Or of the Old Testament wife whose price was above jewels, who supported her husband so he could sit at the town gates and engage in disputations. In the communes described in Washington, the men were engaging in their own thing, whether or not it was remunerative at all, whereas the women, when they worked, had the commonplace jobs—substitute teacher, secretary, telephone operator. In a large proportion of communes, it was the women, doing the work society would pay for, who supplied the stable, on-going income.

One document, a kind of "Can-this-marriage-be-saved" manual, analyzes the dynamics of husband-wife relations and tries to show the wife how she can protect herself and liberate herself from her husband's oppression. The way to achieve this goal includes learning to call the shots as he fires them, that is, to learn to "understand, identify, and explicitly state the many psychological techniques of domination in and out of the home. . . . No woman should feel befuddled and helpless in an argument with her husband. She ought to be able to identify his strategems as he uses them and thus to protect herself against them, to say, you're using the two-cop routine, the premature apology, the purposeful misunderstanding, etc." (We are reminded of the movement a generation ago to help the victims of propaganda disarm the manipulators by giving them names for all the techniques used by them.)

Still, most Movement Women marry. For "even when they admit its [marriage's] many faults, they are convinced that it is the only way to avoid loneliness and insecurity and even terror. . . . [But] there is little reality in the human relations in this society, and least of all in marriage."

Among Movement Women who do not marry, there is no feeling of failure. Some, in fact, positively advocate not getting married and having children, though not necessarily celibacy. For some, living alone, "autonomously in control of her own life" was the ideal solution. For some, female communes. "The commune should be politically rather than socially oriented (liberation, not snagging men, should be the goal) and women should practice self-sufficiency individually and collectively. Possibilities for learning from each other should be exploited, while resisting temptation to fall back on each other for entertainment."

At least some nonmovement women have found communes the answer for a satisfying design for living. The February 1967 issue of *The Church Woman* devoted to the single woman included descriptions of two communities of religious lay women. In 1960 there were 141,141 women living in religious group quarters. Several groups of religious have disbanded as orders and reorganized as community workers, living in urban communes. The idea is not at all uncongenial.

Some Movement Women do advocate celibacy as a way of avoiding the slavery of marriage. ("He offers us marriage . . . and has his slave for life!") Or of achieving serenity. "Celibacy would be worthwhile in order to preserve the quietness—'be still and know that I am God'—needed for graceful loving." Or a way of escaping from male aggression. Or a way of depriving men of control over women.

Certainly not all of the Movement Women subscribe to these extreme views; but enough of them do to make an impact. In a large number of cases the husbands, if not enthusiastic about their wives' views, are open to being convinced. And many, in time, do become convinced. Recently male liberation groups have even begun to form (*Newsweek*, July 20, 1970, 75-76).[1]

Quite aside from the destructive effects on women of marriage as now institutionalized, Movement Women also charge it with performing anti-revolutionary functions for industry and the Establishment. By absorbing the shocks that the world inflicts on men, wives deflect any revolutionary rage the men might otherwise feel.

> Women serve as "lightning rods" for men's frustration at other factors in their environment. This can be especially serviceable for the ruling class. Often it is the man of the family who experiences most directly the real power relationships in the society. . . . When wives play their traditional role as takers of shit, they often absorb their husbands' legitimate anger and frustration at their own powerlessness and oppression. With every worker provided with a sponge to soak up his possibly revolutionary ire, the bosses rest more secure. Chauvinist attitudes help to maintain this asocial system of tension-release.

The birth of children transforms a marriage into a family. It ushers in a panoply of new relationships that have a profound effect on the position of women. For it is the erroneous insistence that the functions of "reproduction, sexuality, and the socialization of children . . . are . . . intrinsically related to each other" that is the key to the subordinate position of women. The path is "maternity, family, absence from production and public life, sexual inequality." Historically valid, perhaps, but not intrinsically so. For the nuclear family as we now know it is only one way to organize these functions. They could be structured in other ways. They could, in brief, "tomorrow be de-composed into a new pattern." And many in addition to Movement Women believe they should be.

Much as Movement Women might like to see the development of the surrogate womb, they do not count on it for the present. The reproductive function is accepted as intrinsically female; and not much can be done to liberate women from it, except to play down its importance.

Although not among their major goals, it may turn out that this under-emphasis on reproduction may constitute a major contribution of the revolution the Movement Women are bringing about. One hears more and more often from young women the following model for their own lives:

> We think one should avoid pregnancy (by abortion if necessary) at this time. If one has talent for dealing with children, she (or he) can work in a nursery school or an orphanage or even set up a child care center. If one has an overpowering need to possess a child of one's own, there are many homeless children and unwanted children soon to be born; there is no need, where the world problem is overpopulation and not underpopulation, to bring still more into the world.

For the child-rearing or socialization function is not the same as the reproductive function; and there is no inherent reason, say the Movement Women, why child rearing should be relegated exclusively to women. "They [reproduction and socialization] are [only] historically, not intrinsically, related to each other in the present modern family." They can be separated and structured differently (Bernard, 1966). Movement Women do not accept the psychiatrists' declaration that some "inner space" in women's "somatic design" for the bearing of children also carries with it "a biological, psychological, and ethical commitment to take care of human infancy." They take seriously W. J. Goode's conclusion that real equality between the sexes will require a radical reorganization of society, a reorganization that relieves women of the exclusive responsibility of child rearing. They are ready for it.

We noted earlier that all the thinking and research embodied in this book presupposed the persistence of the status quo, of present "social arrangements," the current way of structuring not only work but also family function. We have looked at plans, suggestions, and ideas for somehow or other integrating the "two roles of women," which characterize the present sexual specialization of functions. There has been near unanimity about the necessity for providing help with child care—by industry, the community, private co-operatives, whoever—for women who want it. Part-time work programs, interrupted careers and retooling programs, counseling—some proposals have been more humanitarian than others, and some more hard-boiled. Whatever form they took, all were designed to make participation in the labor force easier, all presupposed the existing institutional structure. All took for granted the present sexual differentiation of functions. Whatever else might or might not be "woman's work," at least child care and child rearing were peculiarly, intrinsically, eternally, unchangeably women's functions.

But once the legal proscription of the sexual division of labor is achieved, there is no longer a *logical* ground for the sexual specialization of functions (other than reproduction) either. Movement Women challenge the old assumption. Merely helping women bear the load of child care and child rearing is viewed as inadequate. More, much more, is needed. They zero in on the basic problem as they see it: the nuclear family itself. They are not opposed to the nuclear family per se; they accept the father-mother-child constellation. They are not looking for an amorphous, unstructured, impersonal, irresponsible pattern of parent-child relationship. What they reject is the way this group is supposed to live, the privatized household it is expected to maintain, and the division of labor it is supposed to conform to. They protest the way it is now structured as the basic agency of their exploitation by society. As now set up, "the family. . . is the primary agent of sexual repression in this society. . . . By defining woman primarily within the family. . . . it has deprived her of her humanity. . . . If women are to liberate themselves they must come squarely to grips with the reality of the family."

The diagnosis of the family as the major roadblock to the full emancipation of women is very old. It has been monotonously documented ever since the first industrial revolution. Even before Marx it was recognized as wasteful to the economy as well as limiting to women.

> As a unit of consumption independent homes are uneconomical, not to say wasteful, according to rationalistically-minded reformers who have made the modern home a target of their criticisms for over a century. The pre-Marxist socialist, Charles Fourier, was one of the first to point out the defects of the system, and throughout the 19th and 20th centuries socialists and feminists repeated essentially the same arguments as those he used. The spectacle of millions of separate heating systems, kitchens, and laundries, of millions of women marketing individually and cooking individually and thus missing the advantages of a division of labor and specialization and machine technology, seemed to violate most of the canons of efficiency that were being evolved by business and industry. Fourier himself proposed as a remedy that groups of families combine to live cooperatively in phalansteries or apartment houses with common kitchens which would permit a division of labor. Although the actual experiments with phalanxes were not too encouraging when tried out, the ideal of cooperative living arrangements has persisted, doubtless because it represents a real solution to a pressing problem (Bernard, 1942).

I have already commented on the deteriorating effects of domesticity on the mentality of women.

But no one seemed able to do much about it, although some did try, in communities of one kind or another throughout the nineteenth century. In the current ambience of challenge to all authority, to all collective representation, too all taken-for-granted norms inherited from the past, more and more women are challenging those which have defined their functions in ways that inevitably lead to role conflict and deprive them of opportunities to achieve self-actualization. Movement Women are quick to point out the fatal flaw in the classical analysis: it failed to distinguish between the reproductive and the child-rearing or socializing functions. Such a defect of analysis renders any solution all but impossible.

If the nuclear family as structured were performing well the socializing function assigned to it, an argument might be made for its indispensibility, regardless of its costs to the economy as a whole or to individual women themselves. But it was not. Barrington Moore was therefore willing to examine the idea that the family might not even survive as an institution. His concern was not only for women but for everyone, men and children as well as women. The family as now structured was contrary to the public interest.

Following Bertrand Russell, Moore argued that there are conditions now that "make it possible for the advanced industrial societies of the world to do away with the family and substitute other social arrangements that impose fewer unnecessary and painful restrictions on humanity" (Moore, 1958, p. 162). He felt that obligatory affection among kin was "a true relic of barbarism." The demands made on a modern wife and mother were becoming impossible to meet; children were a burden and their care often degrading and demeaning. (Some Movement Women call it "shitwork.") Nor, contrary to all the clichés, did it even do a good job in child rearing to compensate for its defects. Even in 1958, years before Movement Women arrived on the scene, Moore noted, as many have increasingly done since then, that the troubles of adolescence constituted evidence of the "inadequacy" of the family "in stabilizing the human personality." Like Movement Women, he accused modern students of the family of doing little more than "projecting certain middle-class hopes on to a refractory reality." He called for new and creative ways to rear children that would supply the love and affection we know they require but which the modern family by no means guarantees them. Movement Women concurred: "Ask the children what they think of the institution which supposedly exists for their upbringing, their benefit. All the love between 'man and woman' in the world will not make that tiny unit any less lonely, and less perverted to the child who is raised within it." Moore's indictment took on added force in the 1960's, when the public began to feel an enormous bafflement at the alleged outcomes of the child-rearing practices of the 1940's and 1950's. The behavior of the radical young seemed to document Moore's charges. A young woman with the kind of home and family life that was almost archetypically a model of correct child rearing was blown to bits in a bomb factory; young men from the "best" families turned up in jails on narcotics charges. Alienated youth became stereotypes. "The family" that middle-class people were so assiduously protecting against its critics was, indeed, foundering on a "refractory reality." W. J. Goode (1963), like Moore, agreed that conditions now make possible a radical restructuring of family relations, but he noted that "the family bases upon which all societies rest at present [still] required that much of the daily work of the house and children be handed over to women."

If there were indeed something intrinsic in human beings that made the nuclear family as now structured inevitable, the situation would, of course, be hopeless. But there is not. Kinship groups are very old, as, of course, are units of parents-and-offspring. But families are culturally and especially psychologically defined groups. And the extremely privatized nuclear family as we know it today is, historically speaking, not very ancient.

Philippe Aries asks if we are not "unconsciously overly impressed by the part the family has played in our society for several centuries, and therefore . . . tempted to exaggerate its scope and even attribute to it an almost absolute sort of historical authority?" He thinks so. He argues, in fact, that the concept of the family as we think of it is new.

> In the Middle Ages . . . the family existed in silence; it did not awaken feeling strong enough to inspire poet or artist. We must recognize the importance of this silence; not much value was placed on the family. Similarly we must admit the significance of the iconographic blossoming which after the 15th and especially the 16th century followed this long period of obscurity; the birth and development of the concept of the family.

> This powerful concept was formed around the conjugal family, that of the parents and children. This concept is closely linked to that of childhood. It has less and less to do with problems such as the honour of a line, the integrity of an inheritance, or the age and permanence of a name; it springs simply from the unique relationship between the parents and their children (Aries, 1962, p. 364).

Aries' emphasis on the affectional aspects of the family, it might be noted in passing, was in direct contradiction to the Marx-Engels emphasis on the property aspects, a model on which Movement Women tended to rely. Aries traced the diastolic-systolic pattern of conjugal and consanguineal emphases in the family back to the

Frankish state, noting the impact each had on the relative power of wives. He did not disregard property aspects, but he did not emphasize them either.

We have noted the increasing privatization of the home after the fifteenth century. It paralleled and reflected the increasing privatization of the family.

> In the 18th century, the family began to hold society at a distance, to push it back beyond a steadily extending zone of private life. . . . The modern family . . . cuts itself off from the world and opposes to society the isolated group of parents and children. All the energy of the group is expended on helping the children to rise in the world, individually and without any collective ambition; the children rather than the family [constitute the core]. . . . The family has become an exclusive society (Aries, 1962, pp. 398, 404).

This privatization and isolation of the child-centered family reached almost absurd proportions in the twentieth century—with baneful results. Young people were leaving it as soon as they could (Bernard, 1972). And at least part of the motivation that led women to enter the labor force had to do with escape from the family. For our purposes here, the major relevance lies in the fact that the burden of maintaining this privatized, isolated, and probably unwholesome family fell chiefly on the shoulders of women. They had to be at the service of the children, (if not as chauffeur, then as symbolic anchor) not only when they were infants and preschoolers but also when they were teenagers and even young adults. More and more of them were coming to feel that they'd had it.

We have also referred to evidence from a long-time follow-up study of 400 marriages showing that marriages in which there was a high degree of role differentiation—the wife specializing almost exclusively in domestic roles and the husband in the provider role—tended to deteriorate into "empty shell" marriages. The author of the same study questioned "the extent to which children are well served in a highly differentiated family. . . . In families where the wife also works, it is clear that role differentiation is retarded .with the husband assuming some of the household—i.e., specifically family—tasks. Although direct evidence on this is wanting, it seems reasonable to suggest that the father also continues to share at least some active responsibility for the socialization of all children, not just the first-born. Thus, although the child's interaction with the mother is reduced when she works, his interactions with his parents may not be greatly reduced at all. In other words, the child may have a more balanced set of relationships with his parents in cases where both mother and father work" (Dizard, 1968, p. 74).

Enough of diagnosis, Movement Women were saying. So they, as well as others, translated academic discussion into action. They proposed no longer to just stand there, but to do something. An amorphous set of experiments, proposals, and trials-and-errors began to flood the idea hopper. They have not as yet jelled enough to tell us what is happening or is likely to happen. It will take several years before we fully understand what is happening, but it is quite clear that some kind of revolution is taking place. Whether or not it will conform entirely to the ideals of Movement Women, it is certainly later than most conventional people think, as some of the proposed solutions indicate.

NOTES AND REFERENCES

1. Some husbands willingly babysit so that their wives may attend Movement meetings. One young husband was won over to his wife's point of view when she convinced him of the servility of traditional female role prescriptions. *He* did not want an inferior wife. Another young man, when asked why he preferred the company of Movement Women, replied as though the answer were self-evident: they were more interesting and they contributed more to the relationship than more dependent girls did.

Aries, Philippe, *Centuries of Childhood* (New York: Knopf, 1962).

Bernard, Jessie, *American Family Behavior* (New York: Harper, 1942), p. 519.

———, "The Fourth Revolution," *Jour. Soc. Issues*, 22 (April 1966), pp. 76-87.

———, *The Future of Marriage* (New York: World, 1972), Chapter 3.

Dizard, Jan, *Social Change in the Family* (Chicago: Community and Family Study Center, University of Chicago, 1968), p. 74.

Goode, William Josiah, *World Revolution and Family Patterns* (New York: Free Press, 1963), p. 373.

Moore, Barrington, "Thoughts on the Future of the Family," in *Political Power and Social Theory* (Cambridge: Harvard University Press, 1958), p. 162.

Newsweek, (July 20, 1970), 75-76.

II

Diversity
by Fate and Choice
in Marriage
and Family

5

Parents
Without Partners

E. E. LeMasters

The diversity of traditional family types results not only from conscious choice but also from the many vicissitudes to which families are subject—economic loss, poor health, mental illness, accidents, and just plain bad luck. In this selection, E. E. LeMasters offers an overview of the various kinds of parents without partners. These forms of fractured families are the result of death and also divorce and desertion. There is often a tendency to overlook one-parent families resulting from death because they are judged by some as more "natural" than those caused by desertion or divorce. Most members of society hold a more charitable view of families disrupted by mortality than those disrupted by violations of traditional morality. This attitude suggests that in trying to reach an understanding of the problems of diverse family types, we must be cognizant not only of the structural facts themselves but how they are regarded by the persons involved and by outsiders. Whatever the reasons for the fractured family, there are basic problems of role adaptation and the resolution of different personality demands which are similar to those found in "ordinary" families, plus those additional strains resulting from coping with the problems arising from the atypical parent-child relations.
—GFS

Reprinted with permission from LeMasters, *Parents in Modern America* (Homewood, Ill.: The Dorsey Press) 1970 c., pp. 157-75.

In thinking about parents it is easy to assume a model of what might be termed "the biological parent team" of mother and father. In this model two parents act as partners in carrying out the parental functions. Furthermore, both of the parents are biological as well as social parents. It is this parent team model that is analyzed in most of the chapters in this book.

What is not realized by many observers, especially by parent critics, is the fact that a considerable proportion of contemporary American parents do not operate under these ideal conditions. These parents include "parents without partners" (mostly divorced or separated women, but including a few men also); widows and widowers with children; unmarried mothers; adoptive parents; stepparents; and, finally, foster parents.

Some of the groups in the list above are amazingly large—Simon, for example, reports that in the 1960's in the United States there were about *seven million* children living with a stepparent.[1] This means that approximately one out of every nine children in modern America is a stepchild.

In this chapter we wish to do two things: (1) summarize the statistics on these parental subgroups, and (2) analyze the role complications these parents are confronted with. Some of these parents may actually have certain advantages over so-called normal parents, and where this seems to be the case we will analyze this also.

MOTHERS WITHOUT FATHERS

One of the by now familiar parental types in our society is the mother rearing her children alone. As of 1960 about one household out of ten in the United States was headed by a woman.[2] In an earlier, more innocent America, this mother without father was seen as a heroic figure—a brave woman whose husband had died who was struggling to rear her brood by scrubbing floors, taking in family laundry, and so on. This was the brave little widow of an earlier day.

After the end of World War I, as the divorce rate began to climb, this picture—and this woman—underwent a radical change. With the rapid improvement of American medicine, marriages in the early and middle decades of life were no longer broken primarily by death; now the great destroyers of marriages came to be social and psychological, not biological.

With this shift the public's attitude toward the mother with no father by her side changed drastically—it became ambivalent.

In some cases she might be viewed with sympathy and understanding, if she happened to be your sister or a close friend, but more often she was perceived as a woman of questionable character—either the gay divorcee of the upper social class levels or the ADC mother living off the taxpayers at the lower social class levels.[3] In either case the image was a far cry from that of the heroic little widow of the Victorian era.

Statistically, and otherwise, these mothers without fathers fall into five different categories: divorced, separated, deserted, widowed, and never married. All of these categories overlap, so that some mothers might at some point in their lives occupy all five positions in the list.

Our procedure in discussing these mothers in their parental role will be to identify the generic patterns and problems shared by all of these mothers, and then to look at the relatively unique patterns that cluster about any specific position.

GENERIC FEATURES OF MOTHERS WITHOUT PARTNERS

1. Poverty. It has been estimated that while households headed by a woman comprise only about 10 percent of all U.S. households, they constitute about 25 percent of the families in the so-called poverty group in American society.[4]

In the best study yet published on divorced women, Goode found financial stress to be a major complaint.[5] At any given time approximately 40 percent of the divorced husbands in this study were delinquent in their support payments, a pattern that seems to be nationwide.[6]

Poverty is extremely relative, as is deprivation. A divorced woman receiving even $1,000 a month in support payments may have to reduce her standard of living from what it was before her divorce.

The reasons for the financial difficulties of these mothers are not mysterious or difficult to identify. Most American men cannot afford to support two living establishments on a high level. This is one reason why some support payments are delinquent. The man usually gets involved with at least one other woman, and this costs money.[7] Often his new woman is not well off financially and the man may find himself contributing to her support also.

Since a considerable proportion of divorced women are apparently employed at the time of their divorce,[8] they had what is commonly called a two-income family. The mother may continue to work after the father has left the home, but with two living establishments to maintain, two cars, and so on, the financial situation tends to be tight.

In a study of ADC mothers in Boston it was discovered that these women faced financial crises almost monthly.[9] They coped with these difficult situations by accepting aid from members of their family; by pooling their resources with neighbors and women friends in the same plight; and by occasional aid from a boy friend.

In several counseling cases with divorced women the writer was impressed with the annoying feature of the relative poverty experienced by these women—one woman didn't have the money to get her television set repaired and this created tension between herself and her children. Another woman, who lived in an area with inadequate bus service, could not afford an automobile. Any person in our society can understand how frustrating problems of this nature can be.

2. Role conflicts. Since these women have added the father role to their parental responsibilities they tend to be either overloaded or in conflict over their various role commitments. The presence of a husband-father provides more role flexibility than those women now have—if the mother is ill, or has to work late, the husband may be able to be home with the children.

When these mothers are employed outside of the home, as a sizeable proportion are,[10] the work hours usually conflict with those of the school system. Children leave for school too late, get home too early, and have far too many vacations for the employed mother. There are also childhood illnesses that must be coped with.

It is true that the termination of the marriage has reduced or eliminated the mother's role as wife, but she is still a woman in the early decades of life and men will be in the picture sooner or later. Thus she may not be a wife at the moment but she will soon be a girl friend, and the courtship role may be even more demanding than that of wife.

It is the writer's belief, based on numerous interviews with divorced women, that being the head of a household is, for most women, an 18-hour day, seven days a week, and 365 days a year job. It would seem that only the most capable, and the most fortunate, can perform all of the roles involved effectively.

3. Role shifts. Since the vast majority of the mothers being discussed here—80 to 90 percent—will eventually remarry, they face the difficult process of taking over the father role and then relinquishing it.[11] This is not easy for most of us; once we have appropriated a role in a family system it is often difficult to turn it over to somebody else.

Furthermore, these mothers operate in an unusual family system in that, for an indefinite period, they do not have to worry about what the other parent thinks. They are both mother and father for the time being.

This is not entirely true, of course, in the case of the divorced woman, but it seems to be largely true, even for this group.[12] The departed father starts out with the best intentions of "not forgetting my kids," but a variety of factors tend to reduce his parental influence as time goes on.[13]

One divorced woman talked to the writer about the problem of "shifting gears" in her parental roles: "I found it very difficult," she said. "When my husband and I were first divorced he continued to see the children and participated in some of the decisions about them. Then he moved to another state and we seldom saw him after that—but he did continue to send the support checks.

"At this point," she continued, "I assumed almost all of the parental responsibilities, except for the money sent by my former husband and some advice (of questionable value) that my mother chipped in from time to time.

"And then I met the man I am now married to. At first he stayed out of the children's lives, not being sure how long he and I would be going together. But as we moved toward marriage the children became attached to him and gradually he became a foster father to them. Now he has taken over a considerable amount of parental responsibility and I am back almost to where I was before my divorce—I am just a mother again."[14]

In the study by Hill he analyzed role shifts in a group of families in which the father had been temporarily pulled out of the home for military service. Hill discovered (a) that some of the wife-mothers could not pick up the added responsibility when the father left the home, and (b) that some of the mothers could not relinquish the father role when the husband returned from the service. One has the impression that some of the mothers being discussed here have these same problems.

Once these women have remarried there is a sort of built-in strain in that one of the parents (the mother) is a natural parent while the other (the father) is only a stepparent. This syndrome will be analyzed later in this chapter but it needs to be mentioned here.

4. Public attitudes. These mothers are operating in deviant family situations, and for the most part the community tends to regard them and their children as deviants.[15] Except for the widow, all of these mothers are viewed with some ambivalence in our society. They receive some sympathy, some respect, and some help, but they are also viewed as women who are not "quite right"— they did not sustain their marriage "until death do us part."[16]

The unmarried mother, of course, never had a marriage to sustain and the public has no ambivalence about her; they simply condemn her and that's that.[17]

If these mothers require support from public welfare they will find the community's mixed feelings reflected in their monthly check—the community will not permit them and their children to starve, but it will also not allow them to live at a decent level.[18]

We have now examined some of the generic problems of the one-parent family system, except for the system in which the one-parent is a father, which will be looked at later. Now let us analyze the specific features of the subsystems in the one-parent family.

SPECIFIC FEATURES OF THE SUBSYSTEMS IN THE ONE-PARENT FAMILY

1. The divorced mother. The divorced mother has several advantages over the deserted mother: she at least has had the help of a domestic relations court in spelling out the financial responsibility of the father, also the legal arrangements for custody. In this sense divorce is a lot less messy than desertion in our society.

The divorced mother is also legally free to associate with other men and to remarry if she finds the right person—advantages the deserted woman does not have.

The divorced father, it seems to us, is not in an enviable position in his role as father. He may be happy not to be married to his children's mother any more but he often hates to be separated from his children.[19] In a sense he still has the responsibility of a father for his minor children but few of the enjoyments of parenthood. To be with his children he has to interact to some degree with his former wife—a process so painful that he was willing to have the marriage terminated.

In the unpublished study of 80 divorced men, cited earlier, one of the most frequent regrets expressed by the men was their frustration and concern about their relationship to their children.[20]

The divorced mother has one parental advantage that she shares with all other parents without partners; she does not have to share the daily parental decisions with a partner who might not agree with her strategy. In the Goode study of divorced women, the mothers seemed to think this was an advantage.[21] The parental partner can be of great help if the two parents can agree on how their children should be reared, but when this is not the case one parent can probably do a better job going it alone.

2. *The deserted mother.* It has already been indicated that desertions in our society are more messy than divorces.[22] There are two reasons: (1) desertion is more apt to be unilateral with the decision to pull out being made by one party alone; and (2) there is no court supervision of the desertion process—it is unplanned from society's point of view.

The deserted mother is likely to have more severe financial problems than the divorced mother because support payments have not been agreed upon.

Psychologically, desertion is probably more traumatic than divorce, partly because it is more unilateral but also because it is less planned.[23] To the extent that this is true—and we recognize that the evidence on this point is not conclusive—then the deserted mother is handicapped in her parental role by her emotional upheaval or trauma.

This woman also has other problems; she is legally not free to remarry and in a sense not even free to go out with other men since she is technically still a married woman. These feelings, of course, will tend to reflect the social class and the moral subculture of the particular woman.

3. *The separated mother.* If we assume that most marital separations in modern America have been arrived at by mutual agreement, then this mother has certain advantages over the deserted mother. One disadvantage is that her courtship status is ambiguous; another is that she is not free to remarry.[24] Psychologically, the separated mother should reflect patterns similar to those of the divorced mother: her marriage has failed but she has done something about it and now has to plan for her future life.

4. *The widowed mother.* The one big advantage of this parent is the favorable attitude of her family, her friends, and the community toward her. This tends to be reflected in her self-image, thus giving her emotional support. Once she emerges from the period of bereavement, however, she has to face about the same problems

as the women discussed previously—she probably will have financial problems; she will have to be father as well as mother; she may need to get a job; and eventually she will have to consider whether or not to remarry.

It is difficult to say whether the widowed woman suffers more or less emotional trauma than the women whose husbands are still alive but whose marriages are dead. Both have experienced "death" in one form or another—either psychological or physical.

It is undoubtedly true that some of the marriages of widowed women had also failed before the husband died, but there is no way to discover how large this group is.

5. The unmarried mother. This is not the place to review the status and problems of the unmarried mother in our society—the literature on this woman is quite voluminous.[25] It only needs to be said here that this mother has all of the problems of the women discussed before plus a few of her own. She is more likely to be a member of a racial minority—one of the extra burdens she has to shoulder. She is also more likely to be on public welfare[26]—a major burden in itself in our society. Her chances for marriage are not as gloomy as some people once thought,[27] but her chances for a successful marriage may be more dubious.

The unmarried mother does not have to worry about what her child's father thinks, because in most of the 50 states the unmarried father has no parental privileges except that of child support.[28] As a rule his child may be placed for adoption whether or not he wishes to terminate his parental rights.[29]

The unmarried mother has one dubious advantage over the divorced, the deserted, and the separated mothers. She does not have to juggle the ambivalent feelings of the general public toward her; she knows that they disapprove of her almost unanimously.

We are talking here, of course, of the unmarried mothers who keep their children. Those who give up their children for adoption, and those who terminate their pregnancies via the abortionist, have their own problems which will not be discussed in this book.

It is interesting to note that some women in our society have occupied *all* of the position discussed so far. They have been unmarried mothers, divorced, deserted, separated, and widowed, although not necessarily in that order. We have interviewed two such women and they both were remarkable persons.

One of these women was an unmarried mother at 16, deserted at 18, divorced at 20, widowed at 23, and remarried at 25. Along the way she had accumulated six children and had been separated any number of times.[30]

What impressed us about this woman was not only her lonely journey through the wars of matrimony but her intense concern for the welfare of her children. The general public would undoubtedly have viewed her as a "bad" mother, but our own judgment was that she did quite well with children—her problems were largely with husbands and boy friends. It is too bad that women like this don't write books, for they could tell all of us much that we need to know.

FATHER-ONLY FAMILIES

It has been estimated that approximately 600,000 U.S. families have only a father present in the home at any given time. [31] This figure seems large but is small compared to the 4 to 5 million American families in which only a mother is present.

There seems to be relatively little research data available on these "father-only" families. Since custody of minor children is awarded to the mother in our divorce courts in 90 to 95 percent of the cases, it seems logical to assume that the bulk of these "fathers without mothers" represent either desertion or the death of the mother.

It seems likely that these fathers do not continue indefinitely to rear their children alone, that the majority of them remarry, in which case they would experience the same problems of role shifts discussed earlier for mothers on their own.

It also seems likely that these men experience role conflicts between their jobs, their social life, and their parental responsibility.

It is doubtful that these solo fathers would suffer from poverty to the extent found among solo mothers—but the writer has no data to cite in support of this statement.

The rat race experienced by mothers rearing families without the help of a father would likely be found among these men also; it simply reflects what might be termed "role overload."

Psychologically, judging from case studies to be presented shortly, these men probably suffer from the same syndrome found among mothers who have lost their husbands—loneliness, sorrow, perhaps bitterness, often a sense of failure, plus a feeling of being overwhelmed by their almost complete responsibility for their children. About the only effective treatment for feelings of this nature is to find a new partner and get married—the solution most adult Americans rely on for whatever ails them. These fathers are no exception to this statement.

It would appear that these men have a few problems that would be less likely to bother mothers: the physical care of preschool children and the tasks of home management, such as shopping for food and clothes, preparing meals, doing the family laundry, and cleaning the house. Some men become quite adept at this women's work after awhile, but for others a stove or an iron remains a mystery forever.

CASE STUDIES OF FATHERS WITHOUT MOTHERS

1. Case of desertion. A man of 45 talked to us at length about his struggle to complete the rearing of his three children after his wife had deserted him.

"I came home one night from work and she was gone. A note said that she no longer wanted to live with me and that she thought the children would be better off with me."

"Later on I had a letter from her from California with no return address."

Fortunately, one of this father's children was of high school age and could help with the younger children.

This man says that he went "through hell" for several months —the blow of being deserted, plus the added responsibility for his children, were almost too much for him.

The final solution in this case was the willingness of a widowed sister, with no children of her own, to move in with this family and take over most of the responsibility for the children. After a one year trial this arrangement seemed to be working out.

2. Case of divorce. A man interviewed by the writer had divorced his wife because of an affair she had with a friend of his. Since he felt quite strongly that his wife was not competent to rear their four children, he applied to the court for custody of the children and his petition was approved.

This man was quite definite that he and the children managed better without the mother than they had ever done when she had been present.

"She was always feuding with either me or one of the children. She was moody and negative about life. And she hated any kind of housework. After she left the kids and I got along fine. I did the cooking, they did the housecleaning, and we hired a woman to do the laundry. It worked out just fine."

This man—a remarkable person—even took his four children on a year's tour of Europe after his divorce. Using a combined passenger car and bus they camped all over Europe, settling down in one country for several months so the children could attend school and study a foreign language.

This man has now remarried. He still has custody of the four children and reports that "everything is fine."

3. Case involving the death of a mother. This man talked freely of his life after the death of his wife. He said that since only one of his three children (a boy of 10) was still at home when his wife died he had decided to "bach it"—in other words, he did not attempt to employ a housekeeper, nor did he invite any of his grown children to move back into the family home.

He said, "I felt that the boy and I could manage by ourselves and that we would be better off that way."

This was a small town and many relatives were nearby if help was needed.

This man had been very much in love with his wife and had no desire to remarry.

Eight years after his wife's death, when the boy was ready for college or a job, the father did remarry. He feels that the plan worked out well for both him and the boy—but now that the son is about to leave home the father felt the need for companionship and so he got married.

The writer does not present these cases as being typical. They simply illustrate some of the patterns to be found in the father-only family in our society.

IS THE ONE-PARENT FAMILY PATHOLOGICAL?

Most of us probably assume that the one-parent family is inherently pathological—at least for the children involved. It seems only logical to assume that two parents are better than one—the old adage that two heads are better than one.

In his text on the American family, Bell summarizes several studies that question the assumption that two parents are better than one—judging by the adjustment of the children.[32] This, however, does not say anything about the impact of solo child rearing on the parent, which is the major concern of this book.

If one wishes to debate the number of adults required to socialize children properly the question can be raised: who decided that *two* parents was the proper number? Biologically this is natural enough, but this does not prove its social rightness.

As a matter of fact, a good family sociologist, Farber, has asked the question—"are two parents enough? . . . in almost every human society *more* than two adults are involved in the socialization of the child."[33]

Farber goes on to point out that in many societies a "third parent," outside of the nuclear family, acts as a sort of "social critic"of the child.[34]

In a recent review of the literature on the one-parent family by Kadushin, the data did not seem sufficient to support the hypothesis that the one-parent family is inherently dysfunctional or pathological.[35] It has been demonstrated by Schorr that the one-parent family is considerably overrepresented in the American poverty population and also on our public welfare rolls.[36] This does not prove, however, that these families are inherently dysfunctional; it merely proves that our economic, political, and social welfare systems are not properly organized to provide an adequate standard of living for the one-parent family. A casual drive through many rural areas in America, especially Appalachia and the rural South, will soon demonstrate to an unbiased observer that the mere presence of *two* parents does not assure a decent standard of living for a family in our society.

To prove that the one-parent family is inherently pathological one would have to demonstrate that the system generates a disproportionate amount of personal disorganization. Kadushin's search of the literature did not reveal enough firm research data to support such a conclusion.[37] This, of course, does not prove that one parent in the home is as good as two—it simply says that the research to date is not adequate to answer the question.

It is obvious to any clinician that the two-parent system has its own pathology—the two parents may be in serious conflict as to how their parental roles should be performed; one parent may be competent but have his (or her) efforts undermined by the incompetent partner; the children may be caught in a "double bind" or crossfire between the two parents;[38] both parents may be competent but simply unable to work together as an effective team in rearing their children; one parent may be more competent than the other but be inhibited in using this competence by the team pattern inherent in the two-parent system.

The writer happens to believe that one *good* parent is enough to rear children adequately or better in our society. It seems to us that enough prominent Americans have been reared by widows or other solo parents to prove the point.[39]

It is interesting to note that adoption agencies are taking another look at the one-parent family and that some agencies are now willing to consider single persons as potential adoptive parents.[40]

FOSTER PARENTS

A relatively new type of parent in the United States is the "foster parent" utilized by social work agencies to care for children whose biological parents are unable or unwilling to assume parental responsibility. As of 1962 about 176,000 children were living with foster parents in our society. This represented about 70 percent of all American children being cared for by private and public welfare agencies. [41]

Kadushin points out that foster parents have largely replaced the "children's home" in our society: as of 1923 about 65 percent of the homeless children in the United States were living in institutions built for such children, whereas today over two-thirds are living in foster homes. [42]

This is not the place to review the whole foster home movement, but in view of the increase in foster parenthood in our society in recent decades a few observations are in order. [43]

1. Foster parents have no parental rights. Although about 75 percent of all foster home placements turn out to be permanent—the child never returns to his own parents— the foster parents usually have no right to permanent custody of the child. [44] As a rule they cannot adopt the child, nor can they prevent the agency from taking the child away at any time for any reason. The agency is not required to "show cause" when it decides to remove a child from a foster home; there is no appeal to the courts.

About the only clear-cut right the foster parent has is the right to be paid— about 95 percent of them receive compensation for taking care of the child. [45]

2. The foster parent role is ambiguous. Foster parents are supposed to express instant love or affection for the foster child, but at the same time they are not supposed to become so attached to a child that they cannot give the child up at any time.

Kadushin points out that the foster parent role is quite complex: "Because foster parenthood is an ambiguously defined role," he writes, "its enactment is likely to occasion difficulty." [46]

The role is ambiguous in that it combines a commercial arrangement with an expectation of affection or a willingness to perform beyond the call of duty. When a child is sick the workday is 24 hours, with no overtime from the agency.

The foster parent role is ambiguous in that while the job pays, it does not pay very well—and yet the care of the child is supposed to be first class.

Every natural parent and every adoptive parent knows that nobody could pay enough to properly rear a child—even a million dol-
lars would not cover the heartaches and the anguish experienced by
most parents at one time or another.

The foster parent role is also ambiguous in that what is planned
as a temporary placement may turn out to be permanent, while
a placement that was intended to be permanent may be terminated
in a few days if things don't go well.

It is the writer's belief that the foster parent role is one of the
most complex roles attempted by any parent in our society, and
the research seems to support this belief. [47]

ADOPTIVE PARENTS

As of 1963 about 120,000 children were being adopted annually
in the United States. [48] Of this number almost half (47 percent)
were adopted by relatives. About two out of every 100 children
in our society are reared by adoptive parents. [49]

Unlike the foster parents discussed in the preceding section,
adoptive parents have all of the rights that biological parents have
once the final adoption papers are signed by the court having ju-
risdiction. Adoptive parents not only have the same rights as natural parents, but also the same responsibilities.

In a well-known study of adoptive parents Kirk concluded
that they have "very special" problems– intense worry as to how
the adoption will "turn out," deep feelings of insecurity and/or
inadequacy, apprehension, and so on. [50] Reading this book it
seemed to us that the feelings Kirk found in adoptive parents are
universal reactions to parenthood, not just those experienced by
adoptive parents. [51]

Biological parents never really know how their children will
turn out; most of them feel inadequate and insecure; and almost
all of them are literally frightened when they take their first child
home from the hospital and realize the awesome responsibility
they have assumed– 18 to 21 years of daily responsibility for another human being.

Actually, as we see it, adoptive parents have several advantages over biological parents.

1. They get to choose their child. This may not always be the
case, but at least they can reject a child that they consider grossly
unsuited for them. Biological parents have to accept and keep

what "the Lord sends"–bright, dull, retarded, deformed, beautiful, or otherwise.

2. *Adoptive parents are voluntary parents.* These fathers and mothers do not become parents by accident. The adoption process is such that persons who don't know what they are doing are screened out–they never receive a child. Nobody knows how many children in our society were not actually wanted by their biological parents but the number must be substantial.

3. *Adoptive parents have a probation period and can return the child if necessary.* In most states there is a probationary period of six months to a year in which the adoptive parents can decide whether they wish to assume permanent responsibility for the child. With biological parents the point of no return comes at the moment of conception–except for those willing to seek an illegal abortion.

For the above reasons it seems to the writer that the role of adoptive parents is less complex and less fraught with disaster than some people think. The evidence seems to indicate that the great majority of adoptions in our society turn out reasonably well for both the child and the adoptive parents.[52] Whether this can be said for biological parenthood in our society may be debatable.

THE ROLE OF STEPPARENT

There were about seven million stepchildren in the United States as of the 1960's–this is roughly one child out of nine.[53] This is approximately double the number of stepchildren in this country in 1900. The 1960 decade was the first time in America in which more stepchildren were created by divorce and remarriage than by death. One can visualize the large number of stepchildren when it is realized that some 15 million Americans have now been divorced at one time or another.[54]

Some of the children in these families do not know how to refer to their stepparents–especially so when the father or mother has been married more than twice. One college student, a young man of 20, said to us: "My mother has been married four times. I don't even try to remember the name of her latest husband any more—I just call them by number." Actually, after the second divorce, this boy moved in with his maternal grandparents and he now calls them Dad and Mom.

A college girl said to us: "Do you have to love your stepfather? Mine wants to be real 'buddy buddy' but I can't stand him."

A divorced woman of 35, now remarried, is rearing two sets of children– two from her first marriage and two from her husband's first marriage. She finds the role of stepmother difficult and frustrating. "The other day," she told us, "one of my stepsons didn't do what I had asked him to do. When I corrected him about this he said– 'You're not my *real* mother.' I got mad and belted him one." She went on to say that she also found it difficult when one of the stepchildren accused her of being partial to her own children. This woman finds her second marriage satisfying but she regards the role of stepmother as being perhaps the most difficult job she has ever undertaken– and especially so when there are two sets of children.

Actually, the kinds of situations in which stepparents find themselves are almost endless. In the previous case, for example, if this woman has any children by her second husband there will be *three* sets of children. At this point she is not enthused about this prospect.

A stepmother may find herself rearing a group of children from her husband's first marriage; a stepfather may find himself in the same spot; both may have children with them from a previous marriage; one or both may have had children in more than one previous marriage; they may have children in their new marriage and thus start another set of children; and so forth.

Historically, the role of stepmother has been considered the most difficult parental assignment in Western society. It was no accident that the terrible woman in Cinderella was a stepmother.

Probably the stepmother role is so difficult because the children in our society are closer to their mother than their father, and this means that it is very unlikely that anybody can follow the mother without experiencing some problems.

The following factors can be identified as complicating the stepparent role in our society.

1. The stepparent is following a preceding parent. Stepfathers and stepmothers do not start with the child at birth; they follow a preceding father or mother. If the child's relationship with the first parent was positive, this creates difficulty for the stepparent– he or she has to work his or her way into the charmed circle; but if the preceding relationship was negative this also sets up problems– hostility generated in the earlier relationship may be displaced onto the stepparent.

In many different ways the child will be continuously measuring the new parent against the former parent.

2. Stepparents have a tendency to try too hard. Many college students have referred to this in term papers written for the author in which stepparents were discussed.

It seems that the stepparent is so insecure, so afraid of failure with the child, that the stepfather or stepmother pushes the relationship too fast or too hard. [55] Time is required to heal the wounds left over from the previous parent-child relationship and many stepparents don't give the child enough time.

3. Some stepparents try to replace the former parent. Simon and other writers on the stepparent role emphasize that the new parent should usually not attempt to replace the previous father or mother but should see themselves as a supplement, meeting needs of the child not met by the previous parent.[56] This is especially the case in which the child continues to see his biological father or mother.

4. The complex sets of children to be reared by some stepparents. This was discussed earlier in this chapter, but one can see how easy it would be for a stepfather or a stepmother to favor his or her biological offspring over the stepchildren, and even if no favoritism is involved the child may feel there is. Blood ties are very deep in human society and not all of us can rise above this in complex stepparent situations.

For all of the stated reasons, and more, the stepparent in our society has a difficult role. Simon, who probably has the best book on this subject, takes a positive attitude toward stepparents.[57] She points out that millions of children in modern America would literally have no father or mother to rear them if it were not for stepparents.

SUMMARY AND CONCLUSION

It would seem that a sizeable proportion of American parents operate in situations that are far from ideal– they do not coincide with the dream that most of us have when we start a family.

If one fourth of all marriages in the United States end in divorce, this alone would produce a significant proportion of parents who are either rearing their children alone (those who don't remarry) or are involved in the stepparent role (those who do remarry). If we add to this the families in which a father or mother has died, we get an additional group.

And then, to all of these must be added the unmarried mothers, the separated, and the deserted who are not yet (or even) divorced.

It is not correct to just add all of these categories because almost all of them overlap at some point in time.

The writer believes that a conservative estimate would be that 25 to 35 percent of all American parents perform this role at one time or another under abnormal circumstances. In the famous (or infamous) "Moynihan Report" on the American Negro family, it was estimated that 25 to 50 percent of all black children in the United States live at least some part of their childhood with one or both of their biological parents absent.[58]

Actually, there are many additional deviant parent situations that we have not even mentioned: mothers whose husbands are away from home because of military service; fathers whose occupations keep them away from their children most of the time; parents who are temporarily in a mental hospital or other medical treatment facility—a tuberculosis sanitarium, for example.

It would seem, from the above, that the total number of American parents who face difficult situations in carrying out their parental responsibilities is larger than most of us realize.

An attempt was made in this chapter to analyze the problems of parents who function under deviant or abnormal conditions. The two largest groups seem to be mothers rearing children with no father present and stepparents of both sexes.

The assumed pathology of the one-parent family was questioned, and an attempt was made to estimate the total number of American parents operating under abnormal circumstances.

NOTES

1. See Anne W. Simon, *Stepchild in the Family* (New York: Odyssey Press, 1964), p. 69.

2. Alvin Schorr has an analysis of this data in *Poor Kids* (New York: Basic Books, 1966). See especially pp. 16-22.

One estimate concludes that over six million children in the United States are growing up in fatherless homes. See Elizabeth Herzog and Cecelia Sudia, "Fatherless Homes," *Children*, 15 (1968), 177-182.

3. For an excellent discussion of the changing attitudes toward divorced persons see William L. O'Neill, *Divorce in the Progressive Era* (New Haven: Yale University Press, 1967).

4. Schorr, *op. cit.*, chap. 2, "And Children of the Nation Come First."

5. On the financial problems of divorced women see William J. Goode, *After Divorce* (New York: The Free Press, 1956), chap. 16, "Postdivorce Economic Activities."

6. *Ibid.* See chap. 16 for a discussion of the problem of support payments after divorce.

7. The financial problems of the divorced man were analyzed in a 1968 study conducted by the writer and several graduate students from the School of Social Work, University of Wisconsin. Eighty divorced men were interviewed at length. Financial problems were one of the constant complaints of these men. This study is not yet published.

8. On the employment of wives at the point of divorce, see Goode, *op. cit.*, pp. 71-74.

9. A discussion of the financial crises of ADC mothers may be found in Sydney E. Bernard, *Fatherless Families: Their Economic and Social Adjustment* (Waltham, Mass.: Brandeis University, 1964).

10. For an analysis of the employment of mothers with minor children see F. Ivan Nye and Lois Wladis Hoffman, *The Employed Mother in America* (Chicago: Rand McNally & Co., 1963), pp. 7-15.

11. See Reuben Hill, *Families under Stress* (New York: Harper & Brothers, 1949).

12. Goode, *op. cit.*, chap. 21, discusses some of the post-divorce problems of the father and his children.

13. In the 1968 unpublished study of 80 divorced men cited earlier the lack of contact with their children was one of the problems most often referred to by these fathers.

14. This woman was a professional social worker–hence some of her language is a bit technical.

15. For a discussion of the concept of "social deviation" see Marshall B. Clinard, *Sociology of Deviant Behavior* (New York: Rinehart & Co., 1968 ed.), pp. 3-27.

16. On the attitudes of people toward the divorced person in our society, see Morton M. Hunt, *The World of the Formerly Married* (New York: McGraw-Hill Book Co., 1966), *passim.* See also Goode, *op. cit.*, chap. 17, "Social Adjustment."

17. It is possible, of course, for a woman who was once married to become an unmarried mother at a later date– as a widow or as a divorced woman.

18. See M. Elaine Burgess and Daniel O. Price, *An American Dependency Challenge* (Chicago: American Public Welfare Assn., 1963), for data on how these mothers and their children live. See also Alvin Schorr, *Explorations in Social Policy* (New York: Basic Books, 1968) for a more recent review of the AFDC program.

19. In the 1968 study of divorced men, conducted at the University of Wisconsin, there was frequent concern expressed by the men about the welfare of their children after the divorce.

20. The 80 detailed interviews from this study are not yet fully analyzed since the field work was not completed until June, 1969.

21. See Goode, *op. cit.*, chap. 21, for a discussion of how the divorced women in his sample felt about rearing children after the marriage had been terminated.

22. One of the better discussions of desertion is the paper by William M. Kephart, "Occupational Level and Marital Disruption," *American Sociological Review*, August, 1955. Among other things Kephart believes desertion to be more common than is generally thought. He also found that desertion was by no means limited to the lower socioeconomic levels.

23. The writer has been unable to find any empirical research which compares the psychological trauma of divorce with that of desertion.

24. On the courtship and remarriage problems of divorced and separated women see Jessie Bernard, *Remarriage* (New York: The Dryden Press, 1956); also Goode, *op. cit.*, chap. 19, "Steady Dating, Imminent Marriage, and Remarriage," Hunt, *op. cit.*, also analyzes these problems at length.

25. On the unmarried mother see the following: Clark Vincent, *Unmarried Mothers* (New York: The Free Press, 1961); also Robert W. Roberts (ed.), *The Unwed Mother* (New York: Harper & Row, 1966).

26. Sydney E. Bernard, *op. cit.*, states that women under 35 with no husbands in the household are responsible for more children than are the households headed by men under 35. See also Schorr, *Poor Kids*, p. 21. In chap. 7, "Fatherless Child Insurance," Schorr has an excellent analysis of the economic problems faced by unmarried mothers in our society.

27. See Rose Bernstein, "Are We Still Stereotyping the Unmarried Mother?", *Social Work*, 5 (January, 1960), pp. 22-38.

28. Vincent, *op. cit.*, pp. 73-97, has a discussion of the problems faced by the unmarried father– about whom we really know very little.

29. We hear much about discrimination against women in our society because of their sex. Actually, the unmarried father is discriminated against also. The girl can choose to marry or not and still retain her parental rights, but the man loses his rights as a father unless he marries the girl. Perhaps the unmarried fathers in our society should form an organization and fight for equal rights.

30. This woman was a public welfare recipient.

31. This estimate is by Marjorie Ilgenfritz, "Mothers on Their Own," *Marriage and Family Living*, February, 1961.

32. Robert R. Bell, *Marriage and Family Interaction* (rev. ed.; Homewood, Ill.: The Dorsey Press, 1967), pp. 419-420.

33. Bernard Farber, *Family Orgainzation and Interaction* (San Francisco: Chandler Publishing Co., 1964), p. 457.

34. *Ibid.*

35. Alfred Kadushin, "Single Parent Adoptions: An Overview and Some Relevant Research," May, 1968. Available in mimeographed form from the School of Social Work, University of Wisconsin, Madison, Wisc.

36. See Schorr, *Poor Kids*, chap. 7.

37. Kadushin, *op. cit.*

38. On the "double bind" and its potential impact on children see Virginia Satir, *Conjoint Family Therapy* (Palo Alto: Science and Behavior Books, 1964); also Jay Haley, *Strategies of Psychotherapy* (New York: Grune & Stratton, 1963).

39. This list includes Dr. Nathan Pusey, President of Harvard University, Dr. John Dollard, famous behavioral scientist at Yale University, and John Gardner, formerly Secretary for Health, Education, and Welfare (HEW) in the Johnson Administration.

40. Alfred Kadushin, School of Social Work, University of Wisconsin, a well-known authority on child welfare, says that as of 1967 some adoption agencies began to accept applications from well-qualified single adults. Personal communication.

41. Alfred Kadushin, *Child Welfare Services* (New York: The Macmillan Co., 1967), p. 363. We have relied on this source for child welfare material because when it was published in 1967 it was widely reviewed as being the best analysis of child welfare in the United States yet published.

42. *Ibid.*

43. See Kadushin, *Child Welfare Services,* chap. 9, "Foster Family Care," for an excellent evaluation of foster parent programs in our society; see also David Fanshel, *Foster Parenthood: A Role Analysis* (Minneapolis: University of Minnesota Press, 1966).

44. Kadushin, *op. cit.*

45. *Ibid.,* p. 425.

46. *Ibid.,* p. 396.

47. Both Fanshel and Kadushin agree on the difficulty of the foster parent role.

48. Kadushin, *Child Welfare Services,* p. 437.

49. *Ibid.,* chap. 10, "Adoption," presents a thorough review of the literature on adoption.

50. See H. David Kirk, *Shared Fate* (New York: The Free Press, 1964). While this book is useful, we feel that Kirk would have had more perspective on parental problems if he had compared a group of natural parents with a group of adoptive parents.

51. See E. E. LeMasters, "Parenthood as Crisis," *Marriage and Family Living,* 19 (1957), pp. 352-355. In this study of natural parents having their first child we found about the same apprehension that Kirk found in his adoptive parents. This paper received the Ernest Burgess Award from the National Council on Family Relations.

52. See Kadushin, *Child Welfare Services,* chap. 10, for an evaluation of adoptions in our society. In a well-designed field study in which he followed up adoptions in which the prognosis had not been favorable, Kadushin found that even these adoptions had turned out better than the experts had predicted. See *Follow-Up Study of Older Children Placed for Adoption,* School of Social Work, University of Wisconsin, Madison, Wisc. This study was completed in 1966 and is to be published by the Columbia University Press in 1969 or 1970.

53. Simon, *op. cit.,* chap. 5, "The Child's World Changes," has a detailed review of the statistics on stepparents in our society.

54. Simon, *op. cit.*, p. 59.

55. Simon, *op. cit.*, discusses the problems of stepparents in various chapters. See also Helen Thomson, *The Successful Stepparent* (New York: Harper & Row, 1966).

56. Simon, *op. cit.*, and Thomson, *op. cit.*, *passim.*

57. Simon, *op. cit.*, *passim.*

58. See *The Negro Family*, U. S. Department of Labor, 1965. Although his name does not appear on the report, this document was written by Daniel Patrick Moynihan, hence the label "The Moynihan Report" which has become attached to this study. The report was criticized by various Negro groups when it appeared because of the feeling that Moynihan placed too much emphasis on the problems of the Negro family rather than on the broader social structure of our society. For an interesting analysis of this controversy, see Lee Rainwater and William Yancey (eds.), *The Moynihan Report and the Politics of Controversy* (Cambridge, Mass: M. I. T. Press 1967).

6

Five Kinds
of Relationships

John F. Cuber and Peggy B. Harroff

One of the difficulties in evaluating marriages is that there is such
a wide variation in expectation of what constitutes a satisfactory
relationship. This selection by John Cuber and Peggy Harroff was
chosen because it depicts the wide range of marital styles which
one finds even in one class stratum. They observe that contrary
to commonly held opinion, enduring marriages are not necessarily
synonymous with happy marriages. The Cuber-Harroff typology
is pertinent to our theme of adaptation in a changing society because it shows how different personality types work out diverse
patterns of marriage interaction.   —GFS

* * *

The qualitative aspects of enduring marital relationships vary enor-
mously. The variations described to us were by no means random
or clearly individualized, however. Five distinct life styles showed
up repeatedly and the pairs within each of them were remarkably
similar in the ways in which they lived together, found sexual expression, reared children, and made their way in the outside world.
   The following classification is based on the interview materials of those people whose marriages had already lasted ten years

or more and who said that they had never seriously considered divorce or separation. While 360 of the men and women had been married ten or more years to the same spouse, exclusion of those who reported that they had considered divorce reduced the number to 211. The discussion in this chapter is, then, based on 211 interviews: 107 men and 104 women.

The descriptions which our interviewees gave us took into account how they had behaved and also how they felt about their actions past and present. Examination of the important features of their lives revealed five recurring configurations of male-female life, each with a central theme– some prominent distinguishing psychological feature which gave each type its singularity. It is these preeminent characteristics which suggested the names for the relationships: the *Conflict-Habituated,* the *Devitalized,* the *Passive-Congenial,* the *Vital,* and the *Total.*

THE CONFLICT-HABITUATED

We begin with the conflict-habituated not because it is the most prevalent, but because the overt behavior patterns in it are so readily observed and because it presents some arresting contradictions. In this association there is much tension and conflict-although it is largely controlled. At worst, there is some private quarreling, nagging, and "throwing up the past" of which members of the immediate family, and more rarely close friends and relatives, have some awareness. At best, the couple is discreet and polite, genteel about it in the company of others but after a few drinks at the cocktail party the verbal barbs begin to fly. The intermittent conflict is rarely concealed from the children, though we were assured otherwise. "Oh, they're at it again—but they always are" says the high school son. There is private acknowledgment by both husband and wife as a rule that incompatibility is pervasive, that conflict is ever-potential, and that an atmosphere of tension permeates the togetherness.

An illustrative case concerns a physician of fifty, married for twenty-five years to the same woman, with two college-graduate children promisingly established in their own professions.

> You know, it's funny; we have fought from the time we were
> in high school together. As I look back at it, I can't remember specific quarrels; it's more like a running guerrilla fight
> with intermediate periods, sometimes quite long, of pretty
> good fun and some damn good sex. In fact, if it hadn't been

for the sex, we wouldn't have been married so quickly. Well, anyway, this has been going on ever since. . . . It's hard to know what it is we fight about most of the time. You name it and we'll fight about it. It's sometimes something I've said that she remembers differently, sometimes a decision– like what kind of car to buy or what to give the kids for Christmas. With regard to politics, and religion, and morals– oh, boy! You know, outside of the welfare of the kids– and that's just abstract– we don't really agree about anything. . . . At different times we take opposite sides– not deliberately; it just comes out that way.

Now these fights get pretty damned colorful. You called them arguments a little while ago– I have to correct you– they're brawls. There's never a bit of physical violence– at least not directed to each other– but the verbal gunfire gets pretty thick. Why, we've said things to each other that neither of us would think of saying in the hearing of anybody else. . . .

Of course we don't settle any of the issues. It's sort of a matter of principle *not* to. Because somebody would have to give in then and lose face for the next encounter. . . .

When I tell you this in this way, I feel a little foolish about it. I wouldn't tolerate such a condition in any other relationship in my life– and yet here I do and always have. . . .

No– we never have considered divorce or separation or anything so clear-cut. I realize that other people do, and I can't say that it has never occurred to either of us, but we've never considered it seriously.

A number of times there has been a crisis, like the time I was in the automobile accident, and the time she almost died in childbirth, and then I guess we really showed that we do care about each other. But as soon as the crisis is over, it's business as usual.

There is a subtle valence in these conflict-habituated relationships. It is easily missed in casual observation. So central is the necessity for channeling conflict and bridling hostility that these considerations come to preoccupy much of the interaction. Some psychiatrists have gone so far as to suggest that it is precisely the deep need to do psychological battle with one another which constitutes the cohesive factor insuring continuity of the marriage. Possibly so. But even from a surface point of view, the overt and manifest fact of habituated attention to handling tension, keeping it chained, and concealing it, is clearly seen as a dominant life force. And it can, and does for some, last for a whole lifetime.

THE DEVITALIZED

The key to the devitalized mode is the clear discrepancy between middle-aged reality and the earlier years. These people usually characterized themselves as having been "deeply in love" during the early years, as having spent a great deal of time together, having enjoyed sex, and most importantly of all, having had a close identification with one another. The present picture, with some variation from case to case, is in clear contrast—little time is spent together, sexual relationships are far less satisfying qualitatively or quantitatively, and interests and activities are not shared, at least not in the deeper and meaningful way they once were. Most of their time together now is "duty time"—entertaining together, planning and sharing activities with children, and participating in various kinds of required community responsibilities. They do as a rule retain, in addition to a genuine and mutual interest in the welfare of their children, a shared attention to their joint property and the husband's career. But even in the latter case the interest is contrasting. Despite a common dependency on his success and the benefits which flow therefrom, there is typically very little sharing of the intrinsic aspects of career—simply an acknowledgment of their mutual dependency on the fruits.

Two rather distinct subtypes of the devitalized take shape by the middle years. The following reflections of two housewives in their late forties illustrate both the common and the distinguishing features:

> Judging by the way it was when we were first married—say the first five years or so—things are pretty matter-of-fact now—even dull. They're dull between us, I mean. The children are a lot of fun, keep us pretty busy, and there are lots of outside things—you know, like Little League and the P.T.A. and the Swim Club, and even the company parties aren't so bad. But I mean where Bob and I are concerned—if you followed us around, you'd wonder why we ever got *married*. We take each other for granted. We laugh at the same things

sometimes, but we don't really laugh together—the way we used to. But, as he said to me the other night—with one or two under the belt, I think—"You know, you're still a little fun now and then.". . .

Now, I don't say this to complain, not in the least. There's a cycle to life. There are things you do in high school. And different things you do in college. Then you're a young adult. And then you're middle-aged. That's where we are now. . . . I'll admit that I do yearn for the old days when sex was a big thing and going out was fun and I hung on to every thing he said about his work and his ideas as if they were coming from a genius or something. But then you get the children and other responsibilities. I have the home and Bob has a tremendous burden of responsibility at the office. . . . He's completely responsible for setting up the new branch now. . . . You have to adjust to these things and we both try to gracefully. . . . Anniversaries though do sometimes remind you kind of hard. . . .

The other kind of hindsight from a woman in a devitalized relationship is much less accepting and quiescent:

I know I'm fighting it. I ought to accept that it has to be like this, but I don't like it, and I'd do almost anything to bring back the exciting way of living we had at first. Most of my friends think I'm some kind of a sentimental romantic or something—they tell me to act my age—but I do know some people—not very darn many—who are our age and even older, who still have the same kind of excitement about them and each other that we had when we were all in college. I've seen some of them at parties and other places—the way they look at each other, the little touches as they go by. One couple has grandchildren and you'd think they were honeymooners. I don't think it's just sex either—I think they are just part of each other's lives—and then when I think of us and the numb way we sort of stagger through the weekly routine, I could scream. And I've even thought of doing some pretty desperate things to try to build some joy and excitement into my life. I've given up on Phil. He's too content with his balance sheets and the kids' report cards and the new house we're going to build next year. He keeps saying he has everything in life that any man could want. What do you *do*?

Regardless of the gracefulness of the acceptance, or the lack thereof, the common plight prevails: on the subjective, emotional dimension, the relationship has become a void. The original zest is gone. There is typically little overt tension or conflict, but the interplay between the pair has become apathetic, lifeless. No serious threat to the continuity of the marriage is generally acknowledged, however. It is intended, usually by both, that it continue indefinitely despite its numbness. Continuity and relative freedom from open conflict are fostered in part because of the comforts of the "habit cage." Continuity is further insured by the absence of any engaging alternative, "all things considered." It is also reinforced, sometimes rather decisively, by legal and ecclesiastical requirements and expectations. These people quickly explain that "there are other things in life" which are worthy of sustained human effort.

This kind of relationship is exceedingly common. Persons in this circumstance frequently make comparisons with other pairs they know, many of whom are similar to themselves. This fosters the comforting judgment that "marriage is like this—except for a few oddballs or pretenders who claim otherwise."

While these relationships lack visible vitality, the participants assure us that there is "something there." There are occasional periods of sharing at least something–if only memory. Even formalities can have meanings. Anniversaries can be celebrated, if a little grimly, for what they once commemorated. As one man said, "Tomorrow we are celebrating the anniversary of our anniversary." Even clearly substandard sexual expression is said by some to be better than nothing, or better than a clandestine substitute. A "good man" or a "good mother for the kids" may "with a little affection and occasional attention now and then, get you by." Many believe that the devitalized mode is the appropriate mode in which a man and woman should be content to live in the middle years and later.

THE PASSIVE-CONGENIAL

The passive-congenial mode has a great deal in common with the devitalized, the essential difference being that the passivity which pervades the association has been there from the start. The devitalized have a more exciting set of memories; the passive-congenials give little evidence that they had ever hoped for anything much different from what they are currently experiencing.

There is therefore little suggestion of disillusionment or compulsion to make believe to anyone. Existing modes of association are comfortably adequate—no stronger words fit the facts as they related them to us. There is little conflict, although some admit that they tiptoe rather gingerly over and around a residue of subtle resentments and frustrations. In their better moods they remind themselves (and each other) that "there are many common interests" which they both enjoy. "We both like classical music." "We agree completely on religious and political matters." "We both love the country and our quaint exurban neighbors." "We are both lawyers."

The wife of a prominent attorney, who has been living in the passive-congenial mode for thirty years, put her description this way:

> We have both always tried to be calm and sensible about major life decisions, to think things out thoroughly and in perspective. Len and I knew each other since high school but didn't start to date until college. When he asked me to marry him, I took a long time to decide whether he was the right man for me and I went into his family background, because I wasn't just marrying him; I was choosing a father for my children. We decided together not to get married until he was established, so that we would not have to live in dingy little apartments like some of our friends who got married right out of college. This prudence has stood us in good stead too. Life has moved ahead for us with remarkable orderliness and we are deeply grateful for the foresight we had. . . .
>
> When the children were little, we scheduled time together with them, although since they're grown, the demands of the office are getting pretty heavy. Len brings home a bulging briefcase almost every night and more often than not the light is still on in his study after I retire. But we've got a lot to show for his devoted effort. . . .
>
> I don't like all this discussion about sex— even in the better magazines. I hope your study will help to put it in its proper perspective. I expected to perform sex in marriage, but both before and since, I'm willing to admit that it's a much overrated activity. Now and then, perhaps it's better. I am fortunate, I guess, because my husband has never been demand-

ing about it, before marriage or since. It's just not that important to either of us. . . .

My time is very full these days, with the chairmanship of the Cancer Drive, and the Executive Board of the (state) P.T.A. I feel a little funny about that with my children already grown, but there are the grandchildren coming along. And besides so many of my friends are in the orginizations, and it's so much like a home-coming.

People make their way into the passive-congenial mode by two quite different routes– by default and by intention. Perhaps in most instances they arrive at this way of living and feeling by drift. There is so little which they have cared about deeply in each other that a passive relationship is sufficient to express it all. In other instances the passive-congenial mode is a deliberately intended arrangement for two people whose interests and creative energies are directed elsewhere than toward the pairing—into careers, or in the case of women, into children or community activities. They say they know this and want it this way. These people simply do not wish to invest their total emotional involvement and creative effort in the male-female relationship.

The passive-congenial life style fits societal needs quite well also, and this is an important consideration. The man of practical affairs, in business, government service, or the professions—quite obviously needs "to have things peaceful at home" and to have a minimum of distraction as he pursues his important work. He may feel both love and gratitude toward the wife who fits this mode.

A strong case was made for the passive-congenial by a dedicated physician:

> I don't know why everyone seems to make so much about men and women and marriage. Of course, I'm married and if anything happened to my wife, I'd get married again. I think it's the proper way to live. It's convenient, orderly, and solves a lot of problems. But there are other things in life. I spent nearly ten years preparing for the practice of my profession. The biggest thing to me is the practice of that profession, to be of assistance to my patients and their families. I spend twelve hours a day at it. And I'll bet if you talked with my wife, you wouldn't get any of that "trapped housewife" stuff from her either. Now that the children are grown, she finds a lot of useful and necessary work to do in this community. She works as hard as I do.

The passive-congenial mode facilitates the achievement of other goals too. It enables people who desire a considerable amount of personal independence and freedom to realize it with a minimum of inconvenience from or to the spouse. And it certainly spares the participants in it from the need to give a great deal of personal attention to "adjusting to the spouse's needs." The passive-congenial ménage is thus a mood as well as a mode.

Our descriptions of the devitalized and the passive-congenials have been similar because these two modes are much alike in their overt characteristics. The participants' evaluations of their *present situations* are likewise largely the same—the accent on "other things," the emphasis on civic and professional responsibilities, the importance of property, children, and reputation. The essential difference lies in their diverse histories and often in their feelings of contentment with their current lives. The passive-congenials had from the start a life pattern and a set of expectations essentially consistent with what they are now experiencing. When the devitalized reflect, however, when they juxtapose history against present reality, they often see the barren gullies in their lives left by the erosions of earlier satisfactions. Some of the devitalized are resentful and disillusioned—their bitterness will appear at various points throughout this book; others, calling themselves "mature about it," have emerged with reasonable acceptance of their existing devitalized modes. Still others are clearly ambivalent, "I wish life would be more exciting, but I should have known it couldn't last. In a way, it's calm and quiet and reassuring this way, but there are times when I get very ill at ease—sometimes downright mad. Does it *have* to be like this?"

The passive-congenials do not find it necessary to speculate in this fashion. Their anticipations were realistic and perhaps even causative of their current marital situation. In any event, their passivity is not jarred when teased by memory.

THE VITAL

In extreme contrast to the three foregoing is the vital relationship. The vital pair can easily be overlooked as they move through their worlds of work, recreation, and family activities. They do the same things, publicly at least; and when talking for public consumption say the same things—they are proud of their homes, love their children, gripe about their jobs, while being quite proud of their career accomplishments. But when the close, intimate, confidential, empathic look is taken, the essence of the vital relationship becomes clear: the mates are intensely bound together psychologically in important life matters. Their sharing and their togetherness is genuine. It provides the life essence for both man and woman.

> The things we do together aren't fun intrinsically– the ecstasy comes from being *together in the doing.* Take her out of the picture and I wouldn't give a damn for the boat, the lake, or any of the fun that goes on out there.

The presence of the mate is indispensable to the feelings of satisfaction which the activity provides. The activities shared by the vital pairs may involve almost anything: hobbies, careers, community service. Anything– so long as it is closely shared.

It is hard to escape the word *vitality*—exciting mutuality of feelings and participation together in important life segments. The clue that the relationship is vital (rather then merely expressing the joint activity) derives from the feeling that it is important. An activity is flat and uninteresting if the spouse is not a part of it.

Other valued things are readily sacrificed in order to enhance life within the vital relationship.

> I cheerfully, and that's putting it mildly, passed up two good promotions because one of them would have required some traveling and the other would have taken evening and week end time—and that's when Pat and I *live.* The hours with her (after twenty-two years of marriage) are what I live for. You should meet her. . . .

People in the vital relationship for the most part know that they are a minority and that their life styles are incomprehensible to most of their associates.

> Most of our friends think we moved out to the country for the kids; well– the kids *are* crazy about it, but the fact of the matter is, we moved out for ourselves– just to get away from all the annoyances and interferences of other people– our friends actually. We like this kind of life– where we can have almost all of our time together. . . . We've been married for over twenty years and the most enjoyable thing either of us does– well, outside of the intimate things– is to sit and talk by the hour. That's why we built that imposing fireplace–

and the hi-fi here in the corner. . . . Now that Ed is getting
older, that twenty-seven mile drive morning and night from
the office is a real burden, but he does it cheerfully so we
can have our long uninterrupted hours together. . . . The
children respect this too. They don't invade our privacy
any more than they can help—the same as we vacate the living
room when Ellen brings in a date, she tries not to intrude on
us. . . . Being the specialized kind of lawyer he is, I can't
share much in his work, but that doesn't bother either of us.
The *big* part of our lives is completely mutual. . . .

Her husband's testimony validated hers. And we talked to
dozens of other couples like them too. They find their central
satisfaction in the life they live with and through each other. It
consumes their interest and dominates their thoughts and actions.
All else is subordinate and secondary.

This does not mean that people in vital relationships lose
their separate identities, that they may not upon occasion be ri-
valrous or competitive with one another, or that conflict may not
occur. They differ fundamentally from the conflict-habituated,
however, in that when conflict does occur, it results from matters
that are important to them, such as which college a daughter or
son is to attend; it is devoid of the trivial "who said what first and
when" and "I can't forget when you. . . ." A further difference
is that people to whom the relationship is vital tend to settle disagreements quickly and seek to avoid conflict, whereas the conflict-habituated look forward to conflict and appear to operate
by a tacit rule that no conflict is ever to be truly terminated and
that the spouse must never be considered right. The two kinds
of conflict are thus radically different. To confuse them is to
miss an important differentiation.

THE TOTAL

The total relationship is like the vital relationship with the important addition that it is more multifaceted. The points of vital
meshing are more numerous—in some cases all of the important
life foci are vitally shared. In one such marriage the husband is
an internationally known scientist. For thirty years his wife has
been his "friend, mistress, and partner." He still goes home at
noon whenever possible, at considerable inconvenience, to have
a quiet lunch and spend a conversational hour or so with his wife.
They refer to these conversations as "our little seminars." They
feel comfortable with each other and with their four grown chil-

dren. The children (now in their late twenties) say that they enjoy
visits with their parents as much as they do with friends of their
own age.

There is practically no pretense between persons in the total
relationship or between them and the world outside. There are few
areas of tension, because the items of difference which have arisen
over the years have been settled as they arose. There often *were*
serious differences of opinion but they were handled, sometimes
by compromise, sometimes by one or the other yielding; but these
outcomes were of secondary importance because the primary consideration was not who was right or wrong, only how the problem
could be resolved without tarnishing the relationship. When faced
with differences, they can and do dispose of the difficulties without losing their feeling of unity or their sense of the vitality and
centrality of their relationship. This is the mainspring.

The various parts of the total relationship are reinforcing, as
we learned from this consulting engineer who is frequently sent
abroad by his corporation.

> She keeps my files and scrapbooks up to date. . . . I invariably
> take her with me to conferences around the world. Her fem-
> ininity, easy charm and wit are invaluable assets to me. I
> know it's conventional to say that a man's wife is responsible
> for his success and I also know that it's often not true. But
> in my case I gladly acknowledge that it's not only true, but
> she's indispensable to me. But she'd go along with me even
> if there was nothing for her to do because we just enjoy each
> other's company–deeply. You know, the best part of a va-
> cation is not *what* we do, but that we do it together. We
> plan it and reminisce about it and weave it into our work and
> other play all the time.

The wife's account is substantially the same except that her
testimony demonstrates more clearly the genuineness of her "help."

> It seems to me that Bert exaggerates my help. It's not so much
> that I only want to help him; it's more that I want to do those
> things anyway. We do them together, even though we may not
> be in each other's presence at the time. I don't really know
> what I do for him and what I do for me.

This kind of relationship is rare, in marriage or out, but it does
exist and can endure. We occasionally found relationships so total

that all aspects of life were mutually shared and enthusiastically participated in. It is as if neither spouse has, or has had, a truly private existence.

The customary purpose of a classification such as this one is to facilitate understanding of similarities and differences among the cases classified. In this instance enduring marriage is the common condition. The differentiating features are the dissimilar forces which make for the integration of the pair within each of the types. It is not necessarily the purpose of a classification to make possible a clear-cut sorting of all cases into one or another of the designated categories. All cannot be so precisely pigeonholed; there often are borderline cases. Furthermore, two observers with equal access to the facts may sometimes disagree on which side of the line an unclear case should be placed. If the classification is a useful one, however, placement should *as a rule* be clear and relatively easy. The ease is only relative because making an accurate classification of a given relationship requires the possession of amounts and kinds of information which one rarely has about persons other than himself. Superficial knowledge of public or professional behavior is not enough. And even in his own case, one may, for reasons of ego, find it difficult to be totally forthright.

A further caution. The typology concerns relationships, not personalities. A clearly vital person may be living in a passive-congenial or devitalized relationship and expressing his vitality in some other aspect of his life– career being an important preoccupation for many. Or, possibly either or both of the spouses may have a vital relationship– sometimes extending over many years– with someone of the opposite sex outside of the marriage.

Nor are the five types to be interpreted as *degrees* of marital happiness or adjustment. Persons in all five are currently adjusted and most say that they are content, if not happy. Rather, the five types represent *different kinds of adjustment* and *different conceptions of marriage*. This is an important concept which must be emphasized if one is to understand the personal meanings which these people attach to the conditions of their marital experience.

Neither are the five types necessarily stages in a cycle of initial bliss and later disillusionment. Many pairings started in the passive-congenial stage; in fact, quite often people intentionally enter into a marriage for the acknowledged purpose of living this kind of relationship. To many the simple amenities of the "habit cage" are not disillusionments or even disappointments, but rather are sensible life expectations which provide an altogether comfortable and rational way of having a "home base" for their lives. And many of the conflict-habituated told of courtship histories essentially like their marriages.

While each of these types tends to persist, there *may* be movement from one type to another as circumstances and life perspectives change. This movement may go in any direction from any point, and a given couple may change categories more than once. Such changes are relatively *in*frequent however, and the important point is that relationship types tend to persist over relatively long periods.

The fundamental nature of these contexts may be illustrated by examining the impact of some common conditions on persons in each type.

Infidelity, for example, occurs in most of the five types, the total relationship being the exception. But it occurs for quite different reasons. In the conflict-habituated it seems frequently to be only another outlet for hostility. The call girl and the woman picked up in a bar are more than just available women; they are symbols of resentment of the wife. This is not always so, but reported to us often enough to be worth noting. Infidelity among the passive-congenial, on the other hand, is typically in line with the stereotype of the middle-aged man who "strays out of sheer boredom with the uneventful, deadly prose" of his private life. And the devitalized man or woman frequently is trying for an hour or a year to recapture the lost mood. But the vital are sometimes adulterous too; some are simply emancipated– almost bohemian. To some of them sexual aggrandizement is an accepted fact of life. Frequently the infidelity is condoned by the partner and in some instances even provides an indirect (through empathy) kind of gratification. The act of infidelity in such cases is not construed as disloyalty or as a threat to continuity, but rather as a kind of basic human right which the loved one ought to be permitted to have– and which the other perhaps wants also for himself.

Divorce and separation are found in all five of the types, but the reasons, when viewed realistically and outside of the simplitudes of legalistic and ecclesiastical fiction, are highly individual and highly variable. For example, a couple may move from a vital relationship to divorce because for them the alternative of a devitalized relationship is unendurable. They can conceive of marriage only as a vital, meaningful, fulfilling, and preoccupying interaction. The "disvitality" of any other marriage form is abhorrent to them and takes on "the hypocrisy of living a public lie." We have accounts of marriages which were unquestionably vital or total for a period of years but which were dissolved. In some respects relationships of this type are more readily disrupted because these people have become adjusted to such a rich and deep sharing that evidences of breach, which a person in another type of marirage might consider quite normal, become unbearable.

> I know a lot of close friendships occur between men and women married to someone else, and that they're not always adulterous, But I know Betts — anyway, I personally believe they eventually do become so, but I can't be sure about that. Anyway, when Betty found her self-expression was furthered by longer and longer meetings and conversations with Joe, and I detected little insincerities, not serious at first, you understand, creeping into the things we did together, it was like the little leak in the great dike. It didn't take very long. We weren't melodramatic about it, but it was soon clear to both of us that we were no longer the kind of pair we once were, so why pretend. The whole thing can go to hell fast—and after almost twenty years!

Husbands in other types of relationships would probably not even have detected any disloyalty on the part of this wife. And even if they had, they would tend to conclude that "you don't break up a home just because she has a passing interest in some glamorous writer."

The divorce which occurs in the passive-congenial marriage follows a different sequence. One of the couple, typically a person capable of more vitality in his or her married life than the existing relationship provides, comes into contact with a person with whom he gradually (or suddenly) unfolds a new dimension to adult living. What he had considered to be a rational and sensible and "adult" relationship can suddenly appear in contrast to be stultifying, shallow, and an altogether disheartening way to live out the remaining years. He is left with "no conceivable alternative but to move out." Typically, he does not do so impulsively or without a more or less stubborn attempt to stifle his "romanticism" and listen to well-documented advice to the effect that he should act maturely and "leave the romantic yearning to the kids for whom it is intended." Very often he is convinced and turns his back on his "new hope"—but not always.

Whether examining marriages for the satisfactions and fulfillments they have brought or for the frustrations and pain, the overriding influence of life style—or as we have here called it, relationship type—is of the essence. Such a viewpoint helps the observer, and probably the participant, to understand some of the apparent enigmas about men and women in marriage—why infidelities destroy some marriages and not others; why conflict plays so large a role for some couples and is so negligible for others; why some seemingly well-suited and harmoniously adjusted spouses seek divorce while others with provocations galore remain solidly together; why affections, sexual expression, recreation, almost everything observable about men and women is so radically different from pair to pair. All of these are not merely different objectively; they are perceived differently by the pairs, and are differently reacted to, and differently attended to.

If nothing else, this chapter has demonstrated that realistic understanding of marital relationships requires use of concepts which are carefully based on perceptive factual knowledge. Unfortunately, the language by which relationships between men and women are conventionally expressed tends to lead toward serious and pervasive deceptions which in turn encourage erroneous inferences. Thus, we tend to assume that enduring marriage is somehow synonymous with happy marriage or at least with something comfortably called adjustment. The deception springs from lumping together such dissimilar modes of thought and action as the conflict-habituated, the passive-congenial, and the vital. To know that a marriage has endured, or for that matter has been dissolved, tells one close to nothing about the kinds of experiences, fulfillments, and frustrations which have made up the lives of the people involved. Even to know, for example, that infidelity has occurred, without knowledge of circumstances, feelings, and other essences, results in an illusion of knowledge which masks far more than it describes.

To understand a given marriage, let alone what is called "marriage in general," is realistically possible only in terms of particular sets of experiences, meanings, hopes, and intentions. This chapter has described in broad outline five manifest and recurring configurations among the Significant Americans.

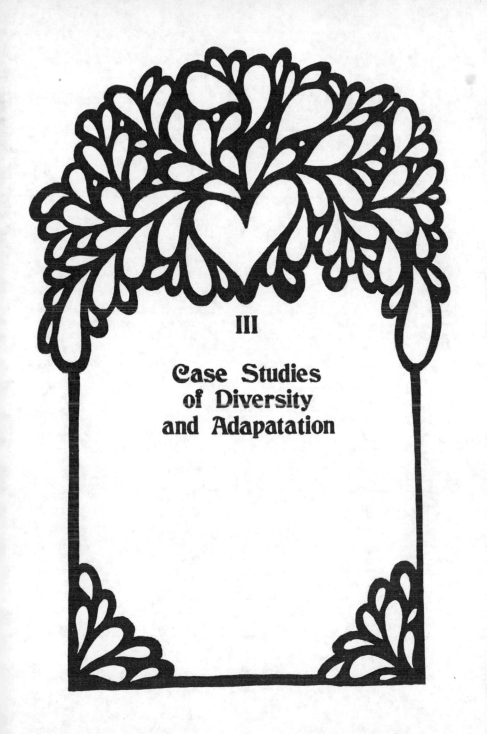

III

Case Studies
of Diversity
and Adapatation

7

Group Marriage: A Possible Alternative?

Albert Ellis

Some of the critics of the isolated nuclear family have suggested group marriage as a possible alternative. In this selection, Albert Ellis makes a balanced assessment of the advantages and disadvantages of this unusual form of marital union.   —GFS

* * *

Is group marriage a possible alternative for the conventional kind of monogamous—or, rather, monogynous marital relationship that now normally exists in Western civilization? Not in the strict sense of the term: if alternative is taken to mean a choice between two things. For it is highly unlikely that group marriage will ever fully replace monogamic mating, or even that the majority of Westerners will voluntarily choose it instead of our present marital system.

This is not to say that monogamy does not have its distinct disadvantages, for, of course, it does. It leads to monotony, to restrictiveness, to possessiveness, to sexual starvation for many unmarried individuals, to the demise of romantic love, and to many other evils. Consequently, it has always tended to be seriously modified by virtually all peoples who have legally adopted it.

From: *The Family in Search of a Future: Alternate Models for Moderns,* Herbert A. Otto, Editor. Copyright © 1970 by Meredith Corporation. Reprinted by permission of Appleton-Century-Crofts, Educational Division, Meredith Corporation.

Thus, in present-day America, we ostensibly marry only one member of the other sex and stay married to him or her for the remainder of our lives. Actually, however, we have very frequent resort to divorce, adultery, premarital sex relations, prostitution, promiscuous petting outside of marriage, and various other forms of non-monogamous sex relations. So our "monogamy" is honored more often in theory than in practice.

Group marriage, however, at least when it is practiced by a relatively small number of people, involves many serious difficulties and disadvantages, and is therefore not likely to become exceptionally popular. Among its distinct shortcomings are these:

1. It is quite difficult to find a group of four or more adults of both sexes who can truly live harmoniously with each other. The usual kind of utopian-minded individual who seeks out such group marriages today is very frequently a highly peculiar, often emotionally disturbed, and exceptionally freedom-loving individual. But group marriage in many ways is not suited to this type of person, because it involves restrictions, restraints, and the kind of self-discipline that he has great trouble in achieving.

2. Even perfectly well-adjusted individuals in our society seem to have difficulty living together successfully in the same household with several other people. Cooperative living of this sort usually involves the scheduling of shopping, cleaning, eating, television-viewing, music-listening, and many other activities at certain times and places which are not going to be particularly convenient to several members of the community-living group. It is often hard enough for two people who love each other to stay together for long periods of time under the same roof, considering that they both are different persons and have all kinds of domestic and other tastes and interests; consequently, many otherwise fairly good monogamic marriages founder. When from four to fifteen people, with even more varying preferences and goals, try to live together continually, many toes are bound to get trod upon and the fur is often likely to fly.

3. Selecting a suitable group of several other individuals with whom one would like to have a group marriage arrangement often proves to be well nigh impossible. It should be remembered, in this connection, that many bright and charming people find it most troublesome to find even a single member of the other sex whom they can fully trust and with whom they would like to settle down to domestic bliss. When these same people go out to

search for several others to "marry" simultaneously, and when they also have to find others who are compatible themselves, it can readily be seen that an enormous selectivity problem arises. Even a highly efficient computer which is fed suitable data on tens of thousands of individuals, and thereby is able to "know" their own characteristics and their likes and dislikes regarding others, will be hard put to select marital groups of, say, four males and four females who can beautifully tolerate—not to mention, love!—each other for a considerable period of time. Simple wife-swapping, as it is sometimes carried on today, where a heterosexual couple try to find another heterosexual couple with whom to swap mates, largely for sexual purposes alone, tends to run into selection troubles, simply because if John and Jane find Hal and Helen, who are both sexually attractive to them, they then have to find that Hal and Helen also find *them* attractive and are willing to swap mates. Because of this selectivity problem, many couples who are quite eager to engage in mate-swapping actually rarely get around to doing so. Imagine, then, how hard it would be for John and Jane, if they wanted to join a group marriage household, to find a suitable Hal and Helen, Matthew and Mary, and Bob and Betty—all of whom would also have to be "sent" by each other!

4. If three or four couples do manage to set up a group marriage arrangement, sex and love problems are almost certain to arise among them. Thus, Jane may get so devoted to Harold that she only wants to be with him or to have sex with him alone. Or Bob may be perfectly potent with Helen and Mary, but not with Jane and Betty. Or Helen may be highly attractive to all the males, while the rest of the girls are not. Or Betty may be the least attractive of the females and may want to have sex relations with the males more than all the other girls do. Or Matthew, who may be the sexiest one of all the males, and the one whose presence really induced most of the females to join the group, may get disenchanted with most of the females and may engage in adulterous affairs outside the group. Or Jane may become so jealous of the other girls, because she thinks they are prettier or more competent than she is, that she may play nasty tricks on them and disrupt the household. All kinds of sex, love, and jealousy problems such as these may easily arise in any sex commune.

5. In our own society, there appear to be fewer females than males at the present time who are interested in group marriage. In Kerista and in hippie groups this phenomenon has often been discovered and has led to the disruption of the groups. Kathleen

Griebe[1] reports that in the utopian community that was established at Walden House a few years ago, difficulty arose on the subject of group marriage, which was favored by the founder of the community, H. Wayne Gourley, and consequently Mr. Gourley had to resign from the organization and sold the house to the remaining members.

Miss Griebe notes that

> group marriage was not defeated at Walden House by a "vote." The simple fact is that there has never been a female at Walden House who had any interest in group marriage. . . . The day when a group of members within Walden House finds itself personally inclined to experiment with group marriage, they will simply do so, without anybody's permission or vote or consensus. Everybody here minds his own business strictly in these matters. In the meantime the idea suffers, as I said from the lack of a single female interested in making the experiment.[2]

Along with these disadvantages of group marriage, there are of course various advantages, including the following:

1. It affords a considerable degree of sexual varietism. If four or more adults get together on a group marriage basis, they all have sexual access to each other; if enough males and females are members of the marital group, two individuals may have intercourse with each other relatively infrequently, even though each of them is having rather frequent sex relations on the whole. This kind of varietism may well serve to keep the participants more sexually alive than they otherwise would be, and to make steady marital relations unusually tolerable.

2. Group marriage widens and enhances love relationships for many individuals. Such people do not merely want to limit themselves to loving one member of the other sex at a given time, but feel that they can intensely love at least several other people. In group marriage, they have the opportunity to relate to, and live with, two or more members of the other sex. Assuming that they can find suitable partners in this respect, they feel much more fulfilled than they otherwise would.

3. Family life can be increased and intensified by group marriage. Instead of merely having one wife and a few children, all of whom may have rather different interests than his own, a man may have several wives and a good many children, some of whom are more

likely to share his own vital absorptions. He may also find it more gratifying, for a number of reasons, to share family life with a relatively large, rather than a relatively small, number of people and may discover that his desires for close kinship are only met in this kind of an unusual manner.

4. Group marriages almost always constitute themselves as some kind of a cooperative living arrangement; this has economic and social advantages for many individuals. Thus, a ménage consisting of, say, six adults and ten children can economically share expenses in a large house; can nicely collaborate on shopping, cooking, cleaning, baby-sitting, and other household tasks; can easily arrange for social contacts and outlets; can work together on their own estate; can own expensive equipment, such as a truck or tractor, that smaller families might not be able to afford; can maintain a good measure of economic security even if some of the adult members are temporarily out of work; and can have many other benefits that would not be easily available to a single couple and their children.

5. Group marriage tends to add an experiential quality to human existence that is likely to be absent or reduced in monogamic mating. Under monogamy (or, for that matter, polygyny) a woman tends to marry at an early age and to have long-term relations with one man and a few children for the rest of her life. Her intense and deep encounters with other human beings, therefore, tend to be quite limited; by the time she dies, it is questionable whether she has ever truly lived. If this same woman participates for a number of years in a group marriage, it is almost certain that she will have multifaceted sex, love, child-rearing, and other human relations that she would otherwise never have, and that she may thereby know herself as a person much better and develop along several fulfilling lines that she easily could have failed to know. And the same thing goes, though perhaps to a lesser degree, for the average male in our society, who today only has one or two monogymous marital experiences.

6. Those individuals who are primarily interested in gaining a sense of the brotherhood of man, and in loving and living cooperatively with a fairly large segment of their surrounding population may partially achieve this goal by participating in a group marriage. In this kind of a situation, they can devote themselves to a larger segment of humanity, in a highly personalized way, than they ordinarily would be able to do, and may find this quite satisfying.

For reasons such as these, it is likely that some individuals will always favor some kind of group marriage, especially in theory, and that some will even find it good in actuality. There seems to be no reason why such people should not be enabled to practice what they preach, since there is no evidence that they will thereby interfere with the rights of others, who want to engage in monogamic, polygamic, or various other types of marriage.

It seems very doubtful, however, that a great many people will rush into group marriages in the near future; it seems even more unlikely that this form of mating and family life will replace monogamy or polygamy on a world-wide or even a national scale. Group sexuality—where three or more adults get together in the same room or in different rooms for the purposes of mate-swapping, heterosexual orgies, bisexual orgies, and other forms of plurisexual combination—has already increased significantly in the United States during the last decade, and is likely to increase more, as men and women become liberated from puritanical notions of what sex should be. It is even possible that within the next fifty years or so most Americans will participate, at some time or other, in some kind of simultaneous sex relationships. But it is highly probable that they will do so on an intermittent or temporary basis, rather than steadily, in the course of a group marriage arrangement.

Group marriage, then, is a logical alternative to monogamic and to other forms of marriage for a select few. In practice, marriage tends to be monogynous (that is, a man and woman living fairly permanently, though not necessarily forever, only with each other and their own children) all over the world, even when other forms of mating are legally allowed. The chances are that this kind of practice will largely continue, but that a sizeable minority of individuals will devise interesting variations on this major theme or else live in thoroughly non-monogamic unions, including group marriage.

NOTES

1. Kathleen Griebe, "Walden House Talks Back," in *Modern Utopian,* vol. 1, no. 2 (1967).

2. *Ibid.,* p. 2.

8

The Swingers

Duane Denfeld and Michael Gordon

The description and analysis of swinging presented in this selection is not the kind one sees in airport newsstands or in drugstore paperbacks. The authors have given a sociological analysis of the major aspects of swinging. Their research indicates that this form of sexual behavior is significant because it is supposedly engaged in to strengthen the marital bonds and not to weaken them. It is this major purpose of swinging that requires a set of rules which tend to support a monogamous marriage and family relations.

The estimate of the numbers of people engaged in swinging seems exaggerated, given the limitations of age, physical attractiveness, affluence, and absence of religious or ethical attitudes which would preclude such activities.

Furthermore, the psychological barriers of sexual jealousy would also reduce the actual number of persons who would use this method to bolster their marriages. In addition, it goes against the goal of treating other human beings as "whole persons" and thus is counter to other ideals of a healthy society.　　　—GFS

From Duane Denfeld and Michael Gordon, "The Sociology of Mate Swapping," *The Journal of Sex Research*, May 1970, Vol. 7, pp. 85-99. Reprinted with permission.

Swinging, or mate swapping, has been a subject that sells "adult reading" paperbacks, but few social scientists have analyzed it. Fortunately, there are a handful of serious studies of the swinging scene. This is not to maintain that we know all we need to know; the analyses available must be viewed as tentative. The findings of the research are problematic because designs have not been employed which allow generalization. Furthermore, some crucial aspects of the phenomenon have been neglected, e.g., what are the characteristics of those who drop out of swinging? We say this not by way of criticism of the research of our colleagues; they are pioneering in an area that involves great technical as well as ethical problems. Our statements are merely intended to qualify what we have to say in the rest of the paper.

Despite the problems cited above, there are studies which provide excellent descriptive data based on participant observation and interviewing. We will use these ground-breaking papers to test the model presented earlier. It is hoped that the important contributions of Symonds, Bartell, the Smiths, and the Breedloves will encourage further research in this area. Before evaluating our model it is necessary to specify the term "swinging," to discuss the emergence and extent of swinging, and the swingers themselves.

SWINGING

One definition of "swinging" is "having sexual relations (as a couple) with at least one other individual." Another definition, and more appropriate for our purposes, is that "swinging" is a husband and wife's "willingness to swap sexual partners with a couple with whom they are not acquainted and/or to go to a swinging party and be willing for both he and his mate to have sexual intercourse with strangers." The latter definition directs our attention to swinging as a husband-wife activity. The accepted term among mate-sharing couples is "swinging"; the term "wife swapping" is objectionable, as it implies sexual inequality, i.e., that wives are the property of husbands.

Swingers, according to Symonds, are not of one mold; she distinguishes "recreational" from "utopian" swingers. The recreational swinger is someone "who uses swinging as a form of recreation"; he does not want to change the social order or to fight the Establishment. He is, in Merton's typology of deviance, an "aberrant." The recreational swinger violates norms but accepts them as legitimate. The utopian swinger is "nonconformist," publicizing his opposition to societal norms.

He also tries to change them. He is generally acknowledged
by the general society to be doing this for a cause rather than
for personal gain.[1]

Swinging, for the utopian, is part of a new life style that empha-
sizes communal living. The proportion of utopians within the
swinging scene has not been determined. Symonds feels that their
number is small. She found the utopians more interesting

> because of their more deviant and encompassing view con-
> cerning the life that they desire to live if it ever becomes
> possible. In some respects, they fall close to the philosophy
> of some hippies in that they would like to retreat from the
> society at large and live in a community of their own kind.[2]

In societal terms, the recreational swinger is a defender of the status quo; the utopian swinger is one who wants to build a new
order.

We are most interested in the recreational swingers, because
their deviation is limited to the sharing of partners; in other areas
they adhere to societal norms. Couples who engage in recreational
swinging say they do so in order to support or improve their marriage. They favor monogamy and want to maintain it.

THE SWINGER

The swingers who advertise and attend swinging parties do not conform to the stereotypical image of the deviant. They have higher
levels of education than the general population; 80 percent of one
study attended college, 50 percent were graduates, and 12 percent were still students. They are disproportionately found in professional and white collar occupations. They tend to be conservative and very straight.

> They do not represent a high order of deviance. In fact, this
> is the single area of deviation from the norms of contempo-
> rary society. The mores, the fears, that plague our generation
> are evidenced as strongly in swingers as in any random sam-
> pling from suburbia.[3]

Every study we looked at emphasized the overall normality, con-
ventionality, and respectability of recreational swingers.

EXTENT OF SWINGING

The number of couples engaged in swinging can at best be roughly
estimated. The Breedloves developed, on the basis of their research,

an estimate of eight million couples. Their figure was based on a sample of 407 couples. They found that less than 4 percent of them placed or replied to advertisements in swinging publications, and in the year prior to publication (1962-1963) of their study, "almost 70,000 couples either replied to, or placed, ads as swinging couples." With this figure as a base they arrived at their estimate of the number of couples who have at one time or another sexually exchanged partners. They further concluded that, conservatively, 2½ million couples exchange partners on a somewhat *regular* basis (three or more times a year).

GETTING TOGETHER

The "swap" or swingers club is an institutionalized route to other swingers, but it is not the only method of locating potential partners. Bartell suggests four ways: (1) swingers' bars, (2) personal reference, (3) personal recruitment, and (4) advertisement. The last method deserves special attention.

Advertisements are placed in underground papers and more frequently in swingers' magazines. The swingers' publications, it has been claimed, emerged following an article in *MR.* magazine in 1956.

> Everett Meyers, the editor of *MR.*, later claimed that it was this article which touched off a flood of similar articles on wife-swapping, or mate-swapping. In any event, *MR.* followed up its original article with a regular monthly correspondence column filled with alleged letters from readers reporting their own mate-swapping accounts.[4]

Publications began to appear with advertisements from "modern marrieds" or swingers who wished to meet other swingers. *La Plume,* established about 1955, has boasted in print that it was the first swingers' magazine. A recent issue of *Select,* probably the largest swingers' publication, had 3,500 advertisements, over 40 percent from married couples. *Select* and *Kindred Spirits* co-sponsored "Super Bash '70' " on April 11, 1970. It was advertised to be "the BIGGEST SWINGDING yet," and featured dancing, buffet dinner, go-go girls, and a luxurious intimate ballroom. Clubs such as Select, Kindred Spirits, Mixers, and Swingers Life have moved beyond the swingers' party to hayrides and vacation trips.

> There are at least a couple of hundred organizations like Select throughout the country. Many of them are very small,

some with only a few members, and many of them are fly-by-night rackets run by schlock guys less interested in providing a service than in making a quick buck. Most, however, are legitimate and, as such, very successful. They have been a major factor influencing the acceleration of the swapping scene.

Our review of the swinging club and magazine market located approximately fifty nationally sold publications. The "couple of hundred" figure reported above may include some lonely hearts, nudist directories, homosexual, and transvestite organizations, some of which serve the same purpose as swingers' publications. They bring together persons with the same sociosexual interests.

A person's first attendance at a swingers' party can be a difficult situation. He must learn the ideologies, rationalizations, and rules of swinging. These rules place swinging in a context that enables it to support the institution of the family. We turn to these rules in the next section.

RULES OF THE GAME

Our model views swinging as a strategy to revitalize marriage, to bolster a sagging partnership. This strategy can be seen in the following findings of the empirical research. Evidence to support the model is divided into four parts: (1) the perception of limitation of sex to the marital bond, (2) paternity, (3) discretion, and (4) marital supportive rules.

1. "Consensual adultery": the perception that sex is limited to the marital bond. Swingers have developed rules that serve to define the sexual relationship of marriage as one of love, of emotion. Some of the Smiths' respondents would answer "no" to questions pertaining to "extramarital sexual experience," but would answer "yes" to questions pertaining to "mate-sharing or comarital relations." Sharing, for the swingers, means that the marriage partners are not "cheating." Swingers believe that the damaging aspect in extramarital sex is the lying and cheating, and if this is removed extramarital sex is beneficial to the marital bond. In other words, "those who swing together stay together." Swingers establish rules such as not allowing one of a couple to attend a group meeting without the other. Unmarried couples are kept out of some groups, because they "have less regard for the marital responsibilities." Guests who fail to conform to rules are asked "to leave a party when their behavior is not appropriate."

For one group of recreational swingers, it is important that
there be no telephone contact with the opposite sex between
functions. Another group of recreational swingers always has
telephone contact with people they swing with, although
they have no sexual contact between functions.[6]

2. Swinging and children. "Recreational swingers are occasionally
known to drop out of swinging, at least temporarily, while the
wife gets pregnant." By not swinging, the couple can be assured
that the husband is the father of the child; unknown or other par-
entage is considered taboo. This reflects a traditional, middle-
class view about the conception and rearing of children.

Swinging couples consider themselves to be sexually avant-
garde, but many retain their puritan attitudes with respect to sex
socialization. They hide from their children their swinging publications. Swingers lock their children's bedrooms during parties
or send them to relatives.

3. Discretion. A common word in the swingers' vocabulary is discretion. Swingers desire to keep their sexual play a secret from
their nonswinging or "square" friends. They want to protect their
position in the community, and an effort is made to limit participation to couples of similar status or "respectability."

Parties in suburbia include evenly numbered couples only. In
the area of our research, singles, male or female, are discriminated against. Blacks are universally excluded. If the party is
a closed party, there are rules, very definitely established and
generally reinforced by the organizer as well as other swingers. . . . Stag films are generally not shown. Music is low key
fox trot, not infrequently Glenn Miller, and lighting is definitely not psychedelic. Usually nothing more than a few red
or blue lightbulbs. Marijuana and speed are not permitted.[7]

The swinging suburban party differs, then, from the conventional
cocktail party only in that it revolves around the sexual exchange
of mates.

4. Swingers' rules. We suggest that the above rules on sex and
paternity are strategies to make swinging an adjunct to marriage
rather than an alternative. Another set of rules or strategies that
is relevant is that dealing with jealousy. Swingers recognize the
potentially disruptive consequences of jealousy, and are surprisingly

successful in minimizing it. The Smiths found that only 34 percent of the females and 27 percent of the males reported feelings of jealousy. Some of the controls on jealousy are: (1) that the marriage commands paramount loyalty, (2) that there is physical but not emotional interest in other partners, (3) that single persons are avoided, and (4) that there be no concealment of sexual activities. The sharing couples

> reassure one another on this score by means of verbal statements and by actively demonstrating in large ways and small that the marriage still does command their paramount loyalty. Willingness to forego an attractive swinging opportunity because the spouse or lover is uninterested or opposed is one example of such a demonstration.[8]

Developing a set of rules to control potential jealousies demonstrates the swingers' commitment to marriage.

CONCLUSION

In this paper we have attempted to account for a new form of extramarital sexual behavior in terms of a sociological model of deviance. We have contended that swinging may support rather than disrupt monogamous marriage as it exists in this society. A review of the volumes of the *Reader's Guide to Periodical Literature* and *The New York Times Index* failed to reveal any articles dealing with this phenomenon in the United States. This would suggest that swinging has not as yet been defined as a social problem in the traditional sense of the word. Thus swinging, like prostitution, despite its violation of the social and, in many cases, legal norms, is permitted a degree of tolerance which would appear to demonstrate the appropriateness of our model.

Finally, it should be said that we make no pretense to having touched upon all the changes that have played a role in the emergence of swinging. Restrictions of space prevented our looking at the larger societal trends that may have been at work here, e.g., feminism, the changing occupational position of women, suburbanization, and so on. Nevertheless, we do feel that we have delineated those issues which are most directly related to it. The validity of our model will be tested by time.

REFERENCES

1. Merton, Robert K. "Social Problems and Sociological Theory," in R. K. Merton and R. A. Nisbet (eds.) *Contemporary Social Problems*. New York: Harcourt, Brace and World, 1966.

2. Symonds, Carolyn. "Pilot Study of the Peripheral Behavior of Sexual Mate Swappers," unpublished Master's Thesis, University of California Riverside, 1968.

3. Bartell, Gilbert D. "Group Sex Among the Mid-Americans," *Jl. of Sex Research,* 1970, 2:113-130.

4. Brecher, Edward M. *The Sex Researchers.* Boston: Little Brown, 1969.

5. Fonzi, Gaelon and James Riggio. "Modern Couple Seeks Like-Minded Couples. Utmost Discretion." Philadelphia, 1969, 60:9, 76-89.

6. Symonds, *op. cit.*

7. Bartell, *op. cit.*

8. Brecher, *op. cit.*

9

The Family
in Collective Settlements
in Israel

Y. Talmon-Garber

Some of the most interesting examples of diversity in the structure
and functioning of the family are found in the collective settlements of Israel. These Kibbutzim are of particular significance because they were established by Israeli settlers with the explicit
goal of creating a new form of the family based upon new kinds
of relations between men and women and between parents and
children within the context of the communal ownership of property and the communal control of production and consumption. It
should be noted that the alterations in traditional family patterns
were made in accordance with the goal of strengthening the group,
not on the basis of individual preferences or gratifications.

While Kibbutzim vary with respect to political ideology, religious orthodoxy, and collective orientation, the family was de-
emphasized in all of them. Social limitations were placed upon the
way in which parents could support and socialize their children,
but traditional socio-emotional ties were left intact, and indeed
some observers think they may have been strengthened. The members of Kibbutzim have gradually made adaptations to the demand
of traditional family ties, perhaps most noticeably in the reestab-
lishment of kinship ties as the settlements have aged. As a unique
social phenomenon, the collective settlements must be studied
carefully by both the advocates and opponents of new forms of
family.   —GFS

From the *International Social Science Journal*, Volume XIV, No. 3, 1962.
Reprinted by permission of UNESCO.

The main features of collective settlements of Kibbutzim[2] are:
common ownership of property, except for a few personal belong-
ings, and communal organization of production and consumption.
Members' needs are provided for by communal institutions on an
equalitarian basis. All income goes into the common treasury; each
member gets only a very small annual allowance for personal expenses. The community is run as a single economic unit and as one
household. It is governed by a general assembly, which meets as
a rule once a week, by a secretariat and by various committees.
The Kibbutzim are an outgrowth of the revolutionary phase of
Jewish immigration to Israel. The ideological urge to migrate to
the new country and establish Kibbutzim in it has not affected
either whole communities or whole kinship groups– it cut through
and disrupted kinship ties. Most immigrants during this phase
were young and unattached. They came to the country unaccom-
panied by parents or relatives, having discarded their former way
of life and their former social setting. The disposition to establish
cohesive communities and relegate the family to a secondary position is closely connected with this process of dissociation from
former ties. The cohesion of the new primary relations, developed
in the youth movements and later on in the Kibbutzim, replaced
the discarded family ties.

Examination of the first stages[3] of the Collective Movement
and the first phases of the development of each Kibbutz reveals
that there is a certain basic imcompatibility between intense collective identification and family solidarity. The members of the
Kibbutz agree voluntarily to subordinate their personal interests
to the attainment of communal goals and to seek self-expression
only through service to their community. The conception of an
all-absorbing task dominates their life and defines every aspect of
it. The devotion to the realization of communal ideals takes pre-
cedence over kinship obligations. The intimate person-to-person
relations, the intense togetherness, the unity which permeates all
contacts, become more significant than family loyalties. The
intense collective identification counteracts any tendency to renew
contacts with relatives outside the Kibbutzim. Relatives who are
not members are by definition outsiders, almost strangers. It is
felt that external ties should not be allowed to interfere with internal unity. The formation of families of procreation in the Kibbutzim introduces a new source of conflict, in this case an internal
conflict. Deep attachment to the family may weaken the primary
group characteristics of the Kibbutz and disrupt its unity. The families may tend to become competing foci of intensive emotional

involvement and to infringe upon devotion to the community.

From its inception the Collective Movement has realized the danger inherent in external contacts and conflicting loyalties and set out to counteract centrifugal tendencies by a redefinition of the position of the family. The Kibbutzim curtailed family obligations and attachments and took over most of its functions. They have evolved many ingenious devices in order to prevent the consolidation of the family as a distinct and independent unit. Delegation of functions to the Kibbutz is the most important aspect of the 'collectivization' of the family during the first phases of the movement. Husband and wife are allotted independent jobs. There is a strict ban on assigning members of the same family to the same place of work. Division of labour in the occupational sphere is based on a denial of sex differentiation. Women participated to a considerable extent in hard productive labour as well as in defence activities. All meals are taken in the common dining hall. Members' needs are provided by communal institutions. Families look after their own rooms but have few other household responsibilities. Thus each mate works in one branch or another and receives his share of the goods and services distributed by the Kibbutz. Interaction between the sexes in the economic sphere occurs on the level of the community as a whole and not directly between mates. There is during this stage a far-reaching limitation of the functions of the family in the sphere of replacement and socialization as well. The birth rate in the Kibbutzim was for a long time below the level of replacement. The Kibbutzim ensured their continuity and growth not so much by natural increase but by means of recruitment of volunteers from external sources. [4]   The physical care and rearing of the children were basically the responsibility of the Kibbutz and not so much of their parents. In most Kibbutzim children live apart from their parents. From their birth on they sleep, eat and later study in special children's houses. Each age group leads its own life and has its autonomous arrangements. Children meet their parents and siblings in off hours and spend the afternoons and early evenings with them. On Saturdays and holidays they stay with their parents most of the time. In most Kibbutzim parents put their young children to bed every night. There are thus frequent and intensive relations between parents and children. The main socializing agencies are, however, the peer age group and the specialized nurses, instructors and teachers. The age group is a substitute for the sibling group. It duplicates the structure of the community and mediates between children and adults. Basically the children belong to the community as a whole. The core of

internal family activities which looms so large in other types of
family has thus diminished considerably. The family has almost
ceased to be an autonomous unit from the point of view of division of labour.

Another important aspect of the process was the change in
internal family relations. The union between spouses did not require the sanction of the marriage ceremony. A couple who maintained a stable relationship for some time and decided to establish
a family applied for a room and started to live together without
any formalities or celebrations. The wedding was usually deferred
until the birth of children and was performed in order to legitimize
them in accordance with the law of the land. Execution of family
tasks was based on the tenet of equality of the sexes and husband
and wife were in many respects interchangeable. Both conjugal
and parent-children relationships were exceedingly non-authoritar-
ian. The dominant pattern of family interaction during this stage
is comradeship on equal terms.

A fairly strong anti-familistic bias is clearly manifested in patterns of informal social relations and leisure-time activities. Members spent most of their free time together. They met every evening in the communal dining hall, in the reading room or on the
central lawn and spent their time in committee work and heated
discussions. Spontaneous community singing and folk-dancing
were the main recreational activities. Public opinion discouraged
constant joint appearance of the couple in public. Husband and
wife who stuck together and were often seen in each other's company were viewed with ridicule. Each member of the family was
likely to have friends of his own. There was little regard for the
family relationships in work allocation. Husband and wife were
often assigned to jobs with different time-tables and consequently
did not see much of each other. There was hardly any family entertainment or family visiting. Members of the family functioned
independently and were pulled in different directions.[5]

It should be noted that while the Kibbutzim limited the functions of the family drastically and emphasized the collective aspect,
they did not abolish the family altogether.[6] Even during the earli-
est phases when the anti-familistic trend was at its strongest the
family remained a distinct unit. While premarital sexual relations
were permitted, there was a clear-cut distinction between casual
sexual experimentation, love affairs and the more durable and publicly sanctioned unions. By asking for a room of their own, the
couple made public their wish to have permanent relations and
eventually have children. Residence in a common bedroom-living

room allocated by the Kibbutz conferred legitimacy on the couple. While children did not actually share a common domicile with their parents, they visited their parents' room every day, and it was their home by reference. The family did not relinquish its communal functions completely either. Parents contributed to the economic support of their children indirectly by working jointly rather than separately. Similarly, though educators were the designated representatives of the Kibbutz rather than of the parents, the parents exercised a direct and continuous influence on the trained personnel in charge of their children. Since children's institutions were not segregated from the community either ecologically or socially, parents were able to supervise closely the way their children were raised there. They exercised considerable direct influence on their children during the time they spent together every day.[7] While interaction of members of the family with each other was in many cases less frequent than interaction with outsiders, internal ties were more continuous, more meaningful and more intense. The emotional ties that bound husband and wife and parents and children were much more intimate and more exclusive than their ties with other members of the community. The family combined physical and emotional intimacy and supplied its members' needs for close personal contacts which were partly independent of their position in the community. By providing unconditional love and loyalty, it insulated its members from communal pressures and enhanced their security.

The extreme limitation of familial functions and relations was most pronounced in the initial phases of the development of the Collective Movement. It is still to be found, though in a less extreme form, in newly-established collectives. The transition from undifferentiated and extremely cohesive communities to more differentiated and less cohesive ones entails a considerable enhancement of the position of the family. The original homogeneity of the initial stage is disrupted by division of labour and by the establishment and growth of families. The community is further differentiated by the crystallization of various groups of settlers that join the core of founders in each community at different stages of its development. The collectives become more tolerant towards differentiation and subdivision and the family is assigned a place among other sub-groups.

The appearance of the second generation is of crucial importance in this context because children are the main focus of segregated family life in the Kibbutzim. Marriage does not entail a redefinition of roles and a new division of labour and does not cause

a clearly perceptible cleavage between the couple and the rest of
the community. The birth of children makes manifest the partial
independence of the family. There emerges a core of specific family duties and the continuity of the family is no longer dependent
only on the vicissitudes of the love relationship between the
spouses. It becomes more safely anchored in their common attachment to their children and their joint responsibilities to them.
The birth of children affects the family in yet another way. The
appearance of the second generation introduces a gradual shift of
emphasis from disruption of intergeneration ties to continuity.
Children are expected to settle in the Kibbutzim founded by their
parents and continue their life work there. The family of orientation is no longer an external and alien influence. Parents and children are members of the same Kibbutz. They live in close prox-
imity and share, at least to some extent, the same ideals. Identification with one's family may thus reinforce identification with the
collective.

The shift of emphasis from discontinuity to continuity in
more differentiated and less cohesive collectives is expressed in a
partial 'emancipation' of the family. The family regains some of
its lost functions in the sphere of housekeeping. Most families
will have their afternoon tea at home with their children. In some
of the Kibbutzim families will often eat their evening meal at home
too. Most families do it only occasionally, as a special treat for
the children, while some eat at home regularly almost every evening. Couples spend a considerable part of their personal allow-
ances on their flats. The housing policy of the Kibbutzim has
changed considerably. While the houses built during the first
phases of the movement were barrack-like and the dwelling unit
consisted of only one room, the typical dwelling unit now consists of a semi-detached flat containing one or two rooms, kitchen-
ette and private sanitary facilities. The flat serves in many cases
as an important symbol of the togetherness of the family and a
physical manifestation of its separateness. Members usually tend
their flat with care and have a strong desire to make it as neat and
as pleasant as possible.

There is a considerable increase of the family's functions in
the sphere of reproduction and socialization. Examination of
demographic data indicates a considerable increase in fertility in
the Kibbutzim. The dwindling of external recruitment sources and
the difficulties experienced by the Kibbutzim in absorption of
new immigrants have greatly enhanced the importance of natural
increase. Emphasis has shifted from recruitment of volunteers

from outside to expansion from within. The family is now called upon to help the Kibbutz to ensure its continuity and growth. Parents tend to take a more active part in the socialization of their children. There is much closer co-operation between nurses, instructors, teachers and parents. Parents help in looking after their young children. They take turns in watching them at night and nurse them when they are ill. They help in the preparation of festivals arranged for the children and attend most of them. There is considerably more parental supervision of the children's behaviour, their choice of friends and their reading habits. Parents try to influence their children's choice of future occupations and insist on their right to be consulted on this matter. Some of the Kibbutzim have introduced a more radical reorganization. Children in these Kibbutzim no longer sleep in the children's houses. They stay with their age groups during the day but return home every afternoon. Duties of child care and socialization have thus partly reverted to the family.

The line dividing internal family activities and external activities has shifted considerably in all spheres except for the occupational sphere. There is considerable pressure to reduce the number of hours that women work in communal enterprises, but only small concessions have been made in this sphere—mothers of babies get more time off from work now and ageing women start to work part-time earlier than the men. The Kibbutzim put the main emphasis on the occupational role and it has remained the major focus of activity for both men and women. Yet even in this sphere we witness considerable modifications. There is now a fairly clear-cut sex-role differentiation in work organization. Women are mainly concentrated in occupations more closely allied to traditional housekeeping such as cooking, laundry service, nursing and teaching.[8]

Modification in patterns of internal family relationships is yet another aspect of the process of change. Marriage normally now precedes the establishment of a family. Most couples attach considerable importance to the wedding celebration and want it to be a memorable event. There are many signs of the emergence of a fairly fixed albeit flexible and fluctuating internal division of labour. Husbands help in household duties, but in most families women do most of the work and it is mainly their responsibility. The husband is regarded as the wife's assistant or temporary stand-in but not as a co-worker on equal terms. There is considerable co-operation and interchangeability in the relationship to the children, yet in spite of a considerable blurring of differences between

the father role and the mother role, there are some signs of differentiation. The mother is as a rule more concerned with the bodily
well-being of the children and takes care of them while they are at
home. She has usually more contact with the children's institutions and the school and supervises the upbringing of her children
there. There are indications that while the wife has more say in
routine matters it is the husband who usually decides on matters
of principle.

The tendency towards a more familistic pattern may also be
discerned in the subtle transformation of informal relations and
leisure-time activities. Free time spent in public has diminished
considerably. Members are not as eager as they used to be to participate in public discussions or attend public meetings. Spontaneous dancing and community singing sessions are rare. Members
tend to retire to their rooms and to stay at home most of the time.
Husband and wife will spend most of their free time together.
They usually sit near each other during evening meals and on all
public occasions. There is a far better co-ordination of work
schedules as well as of vacations and holidays. Families get special
consideration in this respect and are able to spend their free time
together. Entertaining and visiting are becoming joint family affairs. It is now considered impolite to invite only one of the
spouses. Friends who are not congenial to both husband and wife
are gradually dropped. Many families regularly celebrate birth-
days and wedding anniversaries and attach considerable importance
to such family affairs.

In the sphere of parent-children relations we witness an interesting 'dialectical' process. The extreme limitation of the functions of the family in the sphere of maintenance and socialization
of its children has not led to disruption of the family solidarity.
Paradoxically, the curtailment of obligations reinforced rather
than weakened parent-children relationship and enhanced the importance of the emotional ties between them. It is mainly within
the family that both parents and children have intimate relations
unpatterned by their positions in the community and that they are
free from routine duties. The child's position outside the family
is prescribed only to a small extent. He has to compete with his
age peers for a position in his group and for the approval of the
adults in charge of it. All children in the same age group have the
same claim to attention. It is only in the family that they get love
and care which they do not have to share with many others. In so
far as the family has ceased to be the prime socializing agency, it

avoids to some extent the inevitable ambivalence towards the agents of socialization. Parents do not have to play the two-sided role of ministering to the children's needs for care and security on the one hand and of thwarting their wishes in various ways on the other. Parents do not carry the main responsibility for disciplining their children and can afford to be permissive. Examination of our material indicates the over-all importance of parent-children relationships. The children have come very often to occupy the emotional centre of the parents' life. They have become a major preoccupation with most mothers. Young children are deeply dependent and very often overdependent on their parents. The children eventually outgrow this dependence. They become attached to their age mates and drift away to a certain extent from their parents. Parents resent this partial estrangement and will often blame it on the usurpation of communal institutions. Many feel bereaved of function and crave for closer contacts with their children. It is this process which is at the root of recent reorganizations.[9] Parents now emphasize the unity of the family and encourage closer contacts between all its members. Older children are often entrusted with the care of younger ones and there is a considerable amount of interaction between siblings.

Another outstanding feature of the process of change is the gradual development and renewal of wider kinship ties. As long as the generational structure of the Kibbutz remained truncated, most members did not have any kin besides members of their own elementary family living with them in the same community. A gradual process of change sets in when the children of the founders establish families and the Kibbutz develops into a full-scale three-generational structure. The Kibbutzim have in addition accepted social responsibility for ageing or sick parents[10] and transfer many of them to their children in the Kibbutz. Old parents live either in separate blocks of dwellings or in little semi-detached flats adjoining those of their children. Relatives who live in the same community maintain close contacts through frequent visiting and mutual help. There are many indices of the emergence of cohesive kinship groupings. Relatives tend very often to cluster and form united blocks which have a considerable influence on communal affairs. Wider kinship ties serve also as connecting links with the outside world. Members tend to renew their contacts with relatives when they go to town and will invite them to visit them. They accept personal presents from kin and reciprocate by sending farm produce from time to time. The wider kinship category is amorphous and ill defined, but there is quite a strong moral obligation to maintain amicable relations with kin. Kinship ties have thus broken through the self-imposed isolation of the Kibbutzim from outside contacts.

It should be stressed that in spite of the considerable change in the position of the family the Kibbutzim still remain basically non-familistic. The shift from intergenerational discontinuity to continuity attenuates the tension between the family and the Kibbutz but the basic rivalry is still operative. In so far as the family accepts the primacy of collective considerations it may become a valuable ally. Inasmuch as it resents a subordinate position and disputes the authority of collective institutions it is still a potential source of conflict and competition.[11] The Kibbutzim make far-reaching demands on their members. The proper functioning of the Kibbutz depends on the wholehearted identification of members with its aims and ideals. The collectives cannot afford to allow the family to become an independent and self-sufficient unit lest it undermine the primacy of collective considerations. They still fear that if the family is given a free hand it will become the main focus of primary relations and kinship ties will become preponderant over the ties between co-members.

The violent anti-familism of the revolutionary phase has abated but all traces of it have not disappeared completely. It is superseded by a moderate collectivism which regards the family as a useful though dangerous ally. The Kibbutzim control and limit the family and employ it for the attainment of collective goals.

NOTES AND REFERENCES

1. This analysis is based on a research project which was carried out in a representative sample of the Kibbutzim affiliated with one of the four federations of Kibbutzim. The project has combined sociological and anthropological field methods. The data obtained from the questionnaires, from various types of interviews and from the analysis of written materials were examined and carefully interpreted by direct observation. R. Bar Yoseph took an active part in the initial planning. A. Etzioni assisted me in direction of the project in its first stage. The other main research assistants were: E. Ron, M. Sarell and J. Sheffer. M. Sarell and E. Cohen took over from A. Etzioni in the second stage. The main research assistants were: U. Avner, B. Bonne, S. Deshen,

R. Gutman, Shaku, T. Horowitz, U. Hurwitz and Z. Stup.

2. See M. Spiro, *Venture in Utopia,* 1956.

3. For a similar process, see: R. Schlesinger, *The Family in USSR,* 1949; L. A. Coser, 'Some Aspects of Soviet Family Policy', *American Journal of Sociology,* Vol. LVI, No. 5, 1953; K. Geiger, 'Changing Political Attitude in a Totalitarian Society', *World Politics,* Vol. VIII, 1956; N. S. Timasheff, 'The Attempt to Abolish the Family in Russia', in: N. W. Bell and E. T. Vogel (eds.), *A Modern Introduction to the Family,* 1960.

4. See Y. Talmon-Garber, 'Social Structure and Family Size', *Human Relations,* Vol. XII, No. 2, 1959.

5. For a fuller analysis of the process described here, see Y. Talmon-Garber, 'The Family in Collective Settlements', *Transactions of the World Congress of Sociology,* 1957.

6. See M. Spiro, 'Is the Family Universal? The Israeli Case', in: Bell and Vogel (eds.), op. cit., pp. 55-64.

7. See M. Spiro, *Children of the Kibbutz,* 1958; see also R. Bar Yoseph, 'The Patterns of Early Socialization in the Collective Settlements in Israel', *Human Relations,* Vol. XII, No. 4, 1959, pp. 345-60; E. E. Irvine, 'Observations in the Aims and Methods on Child-Rearing in Communal Settlements in Israel', *Human Relations,* Vol. V, No. 3, 1952, pp. 247-75; A. I. Rabin, 'Infants and Children under Conditions of Intermittent Mothering', *American Journal of Orthopsychiatry,* Vol. 28, No. 3, 1958.

8. For a more detailed analysis of the emergence of sex-role differentiation, see Y. Talmon-Garber, *Sex-role Differentiation in an Equalitarian Society,* 1959, mimeographed.

9. See Y. Talmon-Garber, 'The Family and Collective Education in the Kibbutz', *Niv-Hekvutsah,* Vol. VIII, No. 1, pp. 2-52 (in Hebrew). See also H. Faigin, 'Social Behaviour of Young Children in the Kibbutz', *Journal of Abnormal Social Psychology,* Vol. 56, No. 1, 1958; A. I. Rabin, 'Attitudes of Kibbutz Children to Parents and Family', *American Journal of Orthopsychiatry,* Vol. 29, No. 1, 1959.

10. See Y. Talmon-Garber, 'Aging in a Planned Society', *American Journal of Sociology,* Vol. LXVII, No. 3, 1961, pp. 286-95.

11. On the problems caused by the increased influence of the family on the occupational placement of its children see Y. Tal-

mon-Garber, 'Occupational placement of the Second Generation in Collective Settlements', *Megamoth,* Vol. VIII, 1957, pp. 369 ff. (in Hebrew). See also M. Sarell, 'Continuity and Change—The Second Generation in Collective Settlements', *Megamoth,* Vol. XI, 1961, pp. 2-23 (in Hebrew).

10

Communal Living: Economic Survival and Family Life

JOYCE GARDENER

As the following case study shows, Cold Mountain Farm is an interesting contrast to the Kibbutzim of Israel. In recent years there have been many attempts to create collective settlements in the United States. This case is instructive because it sharply delineates the need for a clear-cut ideology and an integrated organization if one aims to create a new society, even on a very small scale. Since the Cold Mountain Farm members were unwilling to impose regulations on the group, they had an immeasurably harder task than the Kibbutzim which carefully prescribed the regulations and practices.

 The author of *Cold Mountain Farm* uses the phrase "tribal feelings" to describe the nature of the sentiments which held the group together for a summer. The economic difficulties and the social strains which emerged in a short period of time indicate the importance of a viable economic base, clear-cut goals and leadership.

 It should also be pointed out that although the Kibbutzim operate in a larger society which is capitalistic, Israeli society is very supportive of its collective experiments. In contrast, there is considerably more hostility to communal settlements in the contemporary United States.

Joyce Gardener, "The Cold Mountain Farm." From *The Modern Utopian* August 1967, Vol. 2. Reprinted with permission of Alternatives Foundation, P. O. Drawer A, Diamond Hgts. Station, San Francisco, California, 94131.

A study of Cold Mountain Farm is most instructive for the
lessons it may teach not only about the difficulties of establishing
utopian settlements as viable economic units but also about the
problems of rearing children in this environment and operating as
a setting for a new form of the family. When friction and tension
grew in the communal living quarters, the members drew apart
into traditional nuclear family groupings.   —GFS

* * *

Given: 450 acres of land, twelve usable for farming or pasture,
the remainder being old, neglected apple orchards (also pear, plum,
and cherry trees) and young woods, in a mountainous upstate New
York dairy-farming area. A beautiful piece of land, with three
running streams in the springtime, but only one good spring for
water in the summer, close to the five-bedroomed house. The
farm is one mile off the main road, at the end of a rugged dirt
road, a mile from the closest neighbor. There is no rent, no electricity, no telephone—and to acquire any of these would be extremely costly.

The Group: Anarchists. Mostly in their twenties, with children
under six. A fluctuating population, up to thirty. About four
couples and one or two single people consider this home. Mostly
former residents of NYC, but some from other parts of the East
Coast. Interrelationships have existed for as long as five years.

History: Goes back two and a half years, to NYC, where a communal loft once existed, with shared dinners and other occasions.
Or back three years, when at least two families shared an apartment together for a few months. Or to last spring and summer,
when a group of NYC anarchists used half an acre of a friend's
land to farm on weekends.

More concretely, June 1966, to a "Community Conference"
at the School of Living in Heathcote, Md., out of which emerged a
new community—"Sunrise Hill"—at Conway, Mass. At least one
person, loosely connected with the NYC anarchists, went to live
there.

The rest of us continued to farm our friend's land on weekends during the summer, meeting at least once a month at different places in the country during the winter—living together
for a few days, getting to know one another better, and making
plans to start our own farm the following spring. Some people
from Sunrise Hill also attended these meetings.

We finally located this place through a friend. About that time, Sunrise Hill was suffering its final collapse—due to internal conflicts—and four people from there eventually would join us.

ONTO THE LAND

Starting a community farm is an incredibly difficult thing. We didn't fully realize this when we began. Setting up a new farm— or rather, rehabilitating an old and neglected one—was at least a season's work. Not to mention compensating for the work which should have been done the previous autumn.

It was still cold, there was occasional snow, the house was difficult to heat, and no one was prepared to move in. The dirt road was all but impassable, we walked the mile through snow and later mud—carrying babies, supplies, bedding, etc.

Meanwhile we had to find a tractor immediately to haul manure for compost heaps. They should have been started the year before as they require three months' time to rot properly and we wanted to farm organically. We'd have to prune the neglected fruit trees within a month, since pruning too late in the season would shock them.

On the many rainy days we had to make the house liveable: build shelves, worktable, bookshelves, a tool shed, a mail box; install a sink; acquire tools and materials. Somehow, whatever needed to be done, there was always someone who knew how to do it or who was willing to find out how. But with each person having some particular responsibility upon himself, there wasn't time to work on group projects.

Well, we had a farm didn't we? All we had to do was go there when it got nice and warm, plow the land, plant our seed, and wait for the vegtables to come. We didn't even have to pay any rent! It was so simple. No rush to get out there while it was still so cold.

Consequently, the farm was completely deserted until the end of April. Then news got out fast (we couldn't help but brag a little), and we found we had hundreds of friends who wanted to "come to the country." So we had to bite our tongues and violate all the laws of lower east side hospitality to avoid creating a youth hostel or a country resort. We lost a lot of friends that way.

Meanwhile, in NYC, an infinite number of conflicts existed growing out of two difficult years of co-existence, trying to work out an ideology based on anarchism-community-ecology-technology in an environment which presented a constant contradiction to it.

We had discouraged the city people. No one came. The land cried out to be tended, but people were preoccupied with their own personal grievances. The farm was all but deserted. The work fell entirely on the shoulders of a few people. Without telephone and often without car, we waited daily for friends and supplies to show up; waiting for reinforcements. Finally three friends arrived from Conway, reassuringly bringing all their worldly goods. The man started out at once, hooking up running water in the house, pruning some apple trees, then driving to a nearby town without a license or proper registration, and spending three days in jail. Soon he bought us a much-needed tractor. It was precisely this tractor (to this day still only half payed for) which shuttled up and down the one-mile dirt road, hauling cow shit (from neighboring farms, who proved surprisingly friendly) and transporting little children to the nearby town in lieu of Hershey bars—and then, as the time to plow grew nigh, flatly refused to budge.

There was absolutely nothing anyone could do. We had to wait for our friend from Florida to return. He was our only mechanic. Days passed and finally a few people started digging their own gardens—such a pathetic task for a farm that hoped to support some thirty people and then give out free food in the city.

But all this time there were small compensations. We had an opportunity now to explore this incredible land, watch the seasons change, see the snow melt and trees slowly push forth buds, see birds moving in and laying eggs; spy on porcupines each night loudly chomping on the house, make friends with cows and four wild horses grazing on neighboring fields, start to know one another in that unique way that only comes from living together.

TRIBAL FEELINGS

Now a few more old friends began to arrive. There was an incredible feeling of warmth, of family. We were becoming a tribe. There were long, good discussions, around the fire, into the night. Slowly, things were beginning to take shape. In those days I loved to look into the "community room," and see a bunch of people sprawled out on cushions around the floor, all so brown, their bodies so well-developed, their faces relaxed, naked or wearing clothes often of their own making. You could always spot someone from the city—by the whiteness of their flesh, the tenseness of their body.

It was my dream—and certainly no one openly disagreed with me—to become a tribe, a family of "incestuous brothers and sisters." Unfortunately, living so close, we probably made love less than when we lived in separate apartments in the city. And there was so much fear and tension in the air about *potential* affairs, that actual lovemaking all too seldom took place, and even physical contact became a rare thing. Even though we created our own environment at the farm, we still carried with us the repressions of the old environment, in our bodies and our minds.

While others were not actually opposed to these ideas, most people didn't feel quite ready for them, and certainly no one else bespoke the same vision. If we could find a form by which our visions could be shared. . . .

INCREDIBLE TRACTOR

Waiting for the tractor to be fixed (it took about a week and a half of hard labor), living our usual lives, making our own bread and yogurt, etc., we spoke to a nearby farmer and learned of a barn full of manure which he paid men to haul away for him. We offered to do it for him free, in exchange for manure to use as compost. He was so overjoyed that he offered to come up and plow our land in exchange for our labor. We thought he was joking, but a couple of days later, we heard a loud and unfamiliar motor coming up the hill, and there was that huge incredible tractor. "Well, where do you want it?" And that's how we got six acres of land plowed and harrowed (later, we would plow a couple of acres ourselves). A couple of days later, we got our own tractor fixed in order to start hauling manure and planting at a furious pace, trying to get the crops in before it was too late. We were already at least a week behind most everyone else in the area . . . in a place with a *very short* growing season.

These people were so overwhelmingly happy to finally have the tractor, after weeks of frustrated waiting and digging by hand, that one person actually planted some forty mounds of zuchini and eighty mounds of acorn squash and several rows of corn in one day, by hand! Then he devised a method whereby he could dig five furrows at a time by building a drag with teeth for the tractor, and installing the three women as weights on the drag, where they could drop onion sets into the rows. That last part didn't work so well (all the onion sets had to be spaced again, by hand), but nonetheless, by the time the other folks got home about a week later, close to an acre of land had been planted.

Now that there were more of us, we were not so close. There was no real sense of community between us. There was

good feeling, but no center, no clear-cut purpose. Some of the
men felt an unfulfilled need to fight. The women felt an unfulfilled need to love.

About this time we undertook—or were overtaken by—what
I consider one of our most challenging feats: trying to assimilate
a young lawyer and his family, including two girls, aged four and
six. Many a group meeting centered around the problem of "the
kids." Because they were breaking out of a sick environment,
their parents felt they needed a maximum of patience and love
and understanding. Others felt they needed simply to be treated
as human beings and that their mother should not repress the an-
ger and frustration which she obviously felt.

Most of us felt we should in fact try to let them work *through*
their hangups and hopefully eventually come out the other side.
Let them yell "penis" and "vagina" at the top of their lungs. Let
them throw Raggedy Anne into the cellar and elaborate upon her
tortures while chanting, "No, you *can't* come out of the cellar!"
all day long. But what no one seemed to be able to endure were
the howls and wails which rose from the lungs of one sister after
the other, time after time, all day long, and particularly on rainy
days, of which there were many, locked up with them in the house
all day long.

Apparently we just weren't strong enough nor healthy enough
ourselves to be able to cope with these children. And their parents, who had had such great hopes of finding in us a healthy environment, soon had to build their own shelter in order to remove
themselves from our environment.

By this time the house had become so generally unbearable
that everyone else as well had decided to move out. Just before
then, there had been twenty adults and ten children—with only
three or four adults and one child sleeping outside—living so close
together in that house. It seemed absurd to try to keep the house
clean (anarchism does not necessarily mean chaos). And the flies
were so bad that if we hung five strips of flypaper fresh each day
in each room, by evening they were dripping with puddles of
gooey flies. It was just barely possible to exist in the midst of all
these copulating multitudes. (We didn't like the idea of using
poison sprays, with all the cats and babies.)

·   And so, in a burst of desperation to escape the noise, children, chaos, flies, tension . . . everybody dropped everything and
for a few days did nothing but work on their own shelters. The
house was almost deserted.

People who get into community too often forget about the importance of solitude. And we were lucky enough to have plenty of land so that everyone could have their own shelter. But personal possessions (especially kitchen stuff), which had originally been pooled with a great sense of communal enthusiasm, were righteously carted off to their owners' shelters.

HOSTILE OUTSIDERS

About this time we started coming into conflict with the outside world. Ever since it got warm, we had all been walking around more or less nude most of the time. Unfortunately, we had to discontinue this most pleasant practice when neighbors started to mention casually that they could "see everything" from their property on the hill, and that "people were talking." Our local reputation was getting progressively worse. There were too many articles in the mass media about hippies, often loosely connected with legalizing marijuana. The local people, who had originally just thought of us as "strange," and had then begun to accept us as old-fashioned organic farmers, could now call us "hippies" and forbid their kids to have anything to do with us.

The local sheriff began to take an interest in us. Whenever we went into town, we were stopped by the cops. And a friendly gas station attendant told us the highway patrol had been told to watch us. It was easy to be paranoid, to imagine their trying to take our kids away for nudity. It was terrible to compromise, but most of us began to wear clothes again. That was a great loss.

ECONOMIC ARGUMENT

I suppose our first and worst economic argument was whether or not to buy chickens. At first, it was incredible how little a problem money had been. Whoever came just threw in whatever they had—$100 or $200 perhaps—and we'd live off that until someone got a tax return, a welfare check, or whatever. We never did spend more than $25 a week on food—even when there were thirty people. But the chicken crisis involved all sorts of things. Did we need eggs (wasn't wheat germ good enough)? Was it morally right to take eggs from chickens; wasn't it cruel to keep chickens caged?—but if we didn't cage them how would we keep them out of the garden? Were we really saving money on eggs, if we had to spend money on the chickens, chicken wire, and all kinds of feed?

Who was going to plant an acre of millet and an acre of corn to feed them? Who would build the chicken coop? This was the first time I remember hearing anyone say, "Well, *I* won't give any money for chickens"—using money as a weapon, a personal source of power. And it wasn't long before money again became a personal possession.

BAD TIMES

I liked the young lawyer and his wife because they often spoke at meetings on a personal level, about how they *felt* about things, while most of our people maintained a kind of cold objectivity, only discussing things external to themselves. It was this lack of "feeling" which brought the lawyer to say that *Cold* Mountain was certainly an apt name for the place. And his wife complained, not unjustly, that there was not enough making of music, not enough dancing, and she felt her joy was being stifled here.

We seemed to have reached an all-time low. We had passed the summer solstice. Our money was all but depleted. We could work at haying for local farmers, but $1/hr. wasn't a hell of a lot. Until now we seemed to have been subsisting mostly on enthusiasm. Now it was hot and even our enthusiasm was gone. There was a general feeling of emptiness. Times were very bad, but we tried to hold on until the times were more favorable. We decided to limit ourselves to just a few staples (rice, oil, powdered milk, soy sauce, flour, salt, soy beans, brewers yeast, molasses, grass—always purchased in huge quantities to save money) and whatever we could get from our environment—at this time of year, dandelion greens, wintergreen and burdock root and, in a little while fresh strawberries, rhubarb and wild leeks. And we'd soon be getting edible weeds from the garden: milkweed, sorrel, lamb's quarters. And then we would discover violet leaves, for salads. Still later, there would be mushrooms, raspberries, currants and blackberries; wild mint, thyme and oregano; green apples, pears and plums—and by then we would be getting at least zuchini, peas and baby onions from the garden.

Then, one morning someone took the shotgun and killed a groundhog. We'd been talking about hunting for a long time, but most of us were vegetarians and meat was a rare sight in these parts (the hunter himself hadn't eaten meat for the last two years!). But that night he cooked up a fine groundhog stew. Which he ate. And that big pot of stew sat on the stove and people thought about it and talked about it and went to bed without dinner. In the middle of the night a couple of us woke up and had a little. Next day some of us had some for lunch. Only four people remained staunch in their vegetarianism, and mostly they didn't condemn the rest. Each of us worked it out in our own way.

Still, the diet wasn't satisfying. Subsistence living was one thing, but we all felt damned hungry. We called a meeting and decided this had a great deal to do with the cooking—which, until then, had been just a matter of chance impulse, so that the task usually fell into the hands of the same people every day. Their boredom with cooking showed up in the quality of their meals. It seemed reasonable enough that if two different people were responsible for the kitchen each day, there would be more interest and variety in cooking, the house would be kept neater and more organized, and it would leave the other people free to concentrate completely on the garden or whatever. At that time we had fourteen adults, so it was pleasant enough to know you only had to cook and clean one day/week.

It's amazing how much this helped. We'd all begun to grow so discouraged with each other and the mess we were living in. We all felt like pigs and everyone blamed the next person. Our morale was sinking fast, the kids were screaming, and we were at each other's throats. Now suddenly the house was clean—spick and span, almost. People smiled at each other again. The meals were delicious. We felt we had been reborn. We'd stuck it out through hard times, and now virtue had its reward.

At that time, four Puerto Rican friends from the city joined us. They emanated new energy and worked hard. And they had a revolutionary spirit which none of us quite had. One would say, "Communism and capitalism—they are both no good. But if I had something like this farm to fight for—why, I would give my life for it." At night you could hear the guitars and there were big fires, and dancing, and singing. The hardest work was over. All we had to do now was weed and mulch. Now we had time to make music.

PUBLICITY

About this time, an article appeared about us in the *East Village OTHER*—without our knowledge or consent—claiming we needed people to help out on the farm (as if we hadn't had enough trouble discouraging people we knew from coming up!). And we were soon flooded with letters, and every two or three days a new visitor would arrive. It created terrible tensions to have to ask them to leave, to tell them it was all a mistake. And then a couple of people we *did* know arrived and announced their intention to move in. Some of us didn't want to live with these people, while others either wanted them to stay or felt we didn't have any right to ask them to leave. We had decided a long time ago that if this happened, each person in the community would just do as he felt best, and there would be no group decisions.

But how can you ask someone that you know to leave—particularly when they've brought all their things and say they have no place else to go? I think this must be a dilemma suffered by all communities. Certainly my way of dealing with it (absolute frank honesty) was far from effective. They just stayed. And stayed. And gradually, for this reason and others, the warmth and trust and sharing between us began to die. Whatever tribal or family feelings we had had were gone.

We weren't ready to define who we were; we certainly weren't prepared to define who we weren't—it was still just a matter of intuition. We had come together for various reasons—not overtly for a common idea or ideal, but primarily because there was supposed to be a "community." Even in the original community, there were people who thought of themselves (and their reason for being here) as being primarily communitarians, or primarily farmers and back-to-the-soil revolutionaries, or primarily political revolutionaries (anarchists) or "tao-archists" for whom farming and community was just one integral part of the totality, or just plain hermits who wanted to live in the woods. All of these different people managed to work together side-by-side for a while, but the fact was that there was really no shared vision.

And then still more people arrived—people we had all been looking forward to seeing. And the house was very full. And there was a lot of confusion. And it was very difficult to cook for that many people. Again, tensions began to mount. There was little money, and now there were three or four pregnant women here, and one or two nursing mothers. Their dietary needs were very specific, and important, and the community was unable to fulfill them. They were forced to fall back on their own resources. In similar ways, one began to feel they couldn't trust the community to meet their needs, to take care of them in an emergency. There was a feeling of general malaise. The garden wasn't being weeded. The grass was growing higher and higher. Everyone felt as if everyone else was irresponsible.

In a community, things happen on such a large scale that you need the cooperation of other people in order to accomplish almost anything. But now one began to feel as if it was easier to do a thing by oneself. It was hot. Laziness had set in, very firmly. The word "failure" was being tossed around a lot. People began to just look after themselves, and to talk as if the only reason they were here was the land. The City suddenly seemed to hold a great attraction, and whenever there was a car going in, it would be filled to capacity. The young lawyer and his family finally left, quietly.

There was one ray of light in these somber times. A new couple arrived, to stay. Nobody knew them when they came, but everyone liked them at once. They brought new energies with them, and they lifted our spirits. Slowly, all the stragglers had left— empty people who had come to fill themselves, sapping our energies, needing to be taken care of and giving nothing at all— and now there were only between four and six couples and a few single people left.

WINTER APPROACHES

So we all lived together, peaceably enough, until one night it was very cold and wet and windy, and we could smell the coming of autumn. Then it was time to begin thinking about what we'd be doing in the winter—staying here, or moving on—and making plans accordingly. Mostly we had to consider the hardship of a very cold winter, no gas or electricity, a one-mile dirt road which would probably be inaccessible because of heavy snow (even during the summer, only jeeps and 4-wheel-drive cars and trucks could climb that road).

There were five couples, three of the women were pregnant, and a fourth was nursing. The babies were due in October, November and February. The first two couples wanted to deliver their own but not take the chance of doing it here. A single girl was already building a small stone house for the winter. Another man intended to live in the big house for the winter. Almost all hoped to be here early next Spring. By this time, two couples and a girl had moved entirely into their own shelters.

The communal garden was a monstrous failure. After the original enthusiasm of planting, hardly anyone cared enough to weed the rows. (Of course, the huge amount of rain this year retarded the growth of the crops and caused the weeds to grow like crazy! and six acres is a hell of a lot of land to weed by hand. If we try again next year, we'll certainly have to get a cultivator.)

At least two acres of garden were lost, either because they weren't weeded adequately, or because they were planted too late and the growing season was too short, or because there wasn't enough sun and there was too much rain, or because of the aphids, or the potato blight. . . .

We didn't become NEW people—we just became physically healthy people. We didn't find a way of sharing our visions (in fact, we didn't even have a conscious understanding of the *need* for such a thing) and we didn't have a shared vision to bring us and hold us together.

We had plowed and begun to plant the earth, but we had not pierced our own ego skins. Decay, stagnation had already set in. I went into the woods to meditate. The woods explained: it was high time we plowed the earth of this community. We must apply the blade to ourselves and cut back the outer skin to expose the pulsating flesh. And then we must harrow and pulverize the outer skin and use our egos for compost. Then, in the new flesh, we must plant the seeds of the people we wish to become.

11

Dropping Out in Manhattan: An Experiment in Middle-Class Fantasy

Colette Dowling

A kind of family adaptation which is rarely reported in the socio-logical literature—downward mobility by well-educated middle-class persons—is the topic of Colette Dowling's article. The problem of economic deprivation is a subject which many persons intellectualize about (when they are not poor). Mrs. Dowling gives an empathic picture of the meaning of economic loss for persons in the upper middle-income strata. One has a better understanding of the challenges and shifts in roles and family priorities which loss of income entails. This family made a conscious decision to reject the security of the corporation world, without realizing how they were "locked in" with the system, particularly by remaining in an urban environment.   —GFS

* * *

A few months ago the *Wall Street Journal* ran a front-page article called "The Great Escape." It told the stories of a number of exec-utives who decided to chuck it all—the credit cards and two-car garages, the Miltowns and martinis, the fifteen commuter hours a week—and head for the hills.

I know how they feel. A year ago, my husband and I de-cided to drop out for some of the same reasons: money without pleasure, work without accomplishment, life without living. The main difference between us and the families described in the *Journal* is that we wanted to stay in New York. Maybe you can make it in, say, Vermont on $7,400 a year. I'm here to tell you that in New York City, it's tricky. We survived on that last year, and we have three children to support—Gabrielle, who is eight, Conor, who is six, and Rachel, who is four. But let me begin more or less at the beginning.

Ed had been working for the Corporation for Public Broadcasting, a non-profit organization funded by Congress to promote non-commercial television. His title was staff writer. His job was publicity—writing press releases and composing quarterly newsletters to tout the activities of the Corporation.

In a series of jobs dealing with activities that were thrice removed from nothing, this one turned out to be the all-time low in Ed's career. He was uncomfortable in it from the beginning. He felt peculiar sitting in his window-walled office on the twenty-ninth floor of Burlington House—the azure carpeting, the white walls, the banks of white hideaway file cabinets, the white Saarinen conference table at which no one ever conferred. It was pure Antonioni. By no stretch of the imagination did he have enough work to fill 40 hours, much less, he felt, to merit his paycheck of $300 a week, plus annuities and other fringe benefits.

He tried to compensate for his lack of work by getting involved in what he thought were the concerns of the Corporation. He made proposals, wrote memos, offered suggestions. But no one wanted to know that they'd hired a man who found it frustrating to have too little to do. All those make-work efforts were viewed as irritants, grit in the blandly working gears of CPB.

So it came as no surprise to anyone when, a year ago, the Corporation re-organized its promotion department, moved it to the Washington office, and didn't invite Ed to come along. And it came as no surprise to me when Ed, who was about to turn 39, announced he'd had it with jobs that were thrice removed from nothing, and that he would move furniture, sling hash, do *anything* for a living, as long as it was uncompromising and outside the corporate setup. I could see what he meant. To tell you the truth, I'd always felt a bit guilty watching him strap himself together before getting on the subway every morning, while I was free to go into the study and write and listen to music. It was an inequity I had never wanted to look at too closely.

In 1969, the year before we dropped out, our income was $26,000. Last year, the tally of checks from our literary agency,

a small construction company, and several furniture-moving out-
fits came to $7,400 before taxes. That's only $217 above what
the Federal Bureau of Labor Statistics defines as a "lower-level"
budget for a family of four living in New York. And we are a
family of five living (still) in Manhattan, the most expensive of
New York's boroughs.

We might have done better moving to a cold-water cottage in
the Catskills, but New York had marked us. We liked schlepping
along Upper Broadway with all the other sandal-shod dropouts in
our neighborhood. We had even grown accustomed to the soft
sulphurous fog that drifts up to West End Avenue from the Hudson
every night, seeping down into our lungs to be emitted in that
hacking, urban cough that tells us we're *alive*, by God.

Also, and more practically, we're both writers. New York
has always seemed the only place for us to live.

Somehow, we figured it was possible. Neither of us cared
about clothes, and now we really didn't need any. (The children
had always had most of their clothes handed down to them by
friends anyhow.) Our basic expenses were low. The rent on our
six-and-a-half-room semi-professional apartment was $211. (It
has since been raised to $231.) We have no car, no country place,
and so far we've had no chronic medical expenses. We've always
preferred wine to whiskey and knew we could make do with
Guild Tavola at $3.65 the gallon, supplemented by an occasional
find, a 99-cent bottle of Côtes du Rhône that's actually drinkable.

Ed has always been a bug on economical food preparation,
having learned the art in France when he was a graduate student.
Now we would simply have to be *more* economical. Sorrel soup
is cheap and delicious, if you have enough bread and cheese to go
with it. So is Portuguese kale-and-chourizo soup, and leek and
potato, and hopping-john, and arroz con pollo. We were already
hooked on the advantages, both economic and nutritional, of
health food breakfasts: Familia, or Vita Grain, or that prizefighter
of organic cereals, Crunchy Granola.

The days of our liberation began in the spring of 1970 and
ripened with the summer. Ed planned to do some research on a
book. He'd gotten $600 in severance pay (the nonprofit status of
the Corporation made him ineligible for unemployment insurance),
and that would cover the rent for a few months. The kids went to
a city-funded day camp at P.S. 163, from nine to four each day.
Although most of the kids in the camp are black and Puerto
Rican, and the program was doubtless intended to enrich the sum-

mer vacations of children whose parents are poor, no financial
questions were asked of any of the middle-class whites who wanted
to enroll their children. The total tuition of $50 for the summer
for all three of my kids covered hot lunches and trips to city pools
and state lakes. Thus I was free to finish the manuscript my book
publisher had been hounding me for. We were also free for other
things. Simple provolone lunches on the grass in Riverside Park.
A sunny walk to the Columbia bookstore at ten o'clock in the
morning. Early to bed and early to rise. A kielbasa in every other
pot.

From the start, however, the kielbasa had to be worked for.
As is probably not uncommon among people who are relatively
young and relatively affluent, we hadn't saved a cent. And we had
debts. Our income had risen significantly every year, and as our
money had grown, so had the delusion of our security. Security
is a fragile idea with different connotations for everyone. For us
it used to mean the feeling that there'd always be enough money
coming in from somewhere to meet expenses. We always seemed
to have a loan going, though, because when April came we were
never prepared for the amount of untaxed free-lance income we'd
racked up in addition to Ed's salary. Money management, as you
can see, was not exactly our forte.

Thus, when we decided to reject the corporation world that
had fed us so nicely, we had no nest egg to tide us over. That's
another difference between us and those executives in the *Wall
Street Journal.* One of them was a CIA man in his forties who
dropped out, after twenty years, with a severance allotment of
$20,000 in cash. Compared with something like that, our break
was strictly cold turkey. Besides the $600 we'd put aside for rent,
we literally didn't have a cent. Moreover, we owed money to the
bank ($65 a month), to a couple of dentists, to Eastern Airlines
(for a fly-now-pay-later trip to Puerto Rico we'd charged a year
earlier and on which we were paying monthly installments of $14),
and to a psychiatrist we used to go to who'd permitted us to let
our weekly group therapy bills slide, on the obviously shaky ground
that, after a year with him, we'd be making money like bandits.

On April 1, 1970, his first day of freedom, Ed alerted the owners of some Village moving companies that he was available to work
whenever they needed him. I'd say Ed averaged three days of work
a week, at $3 an hour, plus tips. The moving man's work day of-
ten stretches out to twelve or fourteen hours. Two long days of
moving pianos and washing machines, and you're ready to collapse
for the next two. But if a call comes for work at 6 a.m. the next

day, you don't stay in bed, you work. Non-union movers can't afford to turn down a day of work because they never know when the next one's coming.

So food and utilities, last summer, were paid for by the sweat of Ed's brow. The sweat of my own brow produced nothing, save the fulfillment of a professional commitment. It took me three months of working ten hours a day, seven days a week, to honor the contract for a book that might make us some money, someday, but certainly wasn't doing anything for us at the moment. It began to come to me that as a married lady writer, I'd had it easy. I'd never had to view my work as being connected in any way with financial need. Suddenly the connection was there, and it was crucial.

In mid-September I got a check for $1,350, the final payment on my book advance and the first money I'd made since the spring. I saw it go into the bank one day and out the next, in checks to the landlord (two months' rent), the phone company (long distance research calls accounted for a staggering bill), and to Automated Medical Collections for a $275 root canal job I'd had done *before* The Liberation.

Having destroyed for ourselves the option of making easy money, having no medical insurance and no savings to fall back on should a crisis occur, we began to identify viscerally with the so called economically deprived. There's a qualitative difference between gut poverty and the intellectual's distant and more comfortable concern for the poor. Being poor changes the way you see everything.

It changes the way you read the newspaper. You stop looking at the ads. After a while, you simply don't *see* them anymore. It's a psychological trick, at first consciously employed and later automatic, to save yourself from the conflict of knowing you can't have the things that are available to others.

It changes the way you listen to music. Bob Dylan, always "interesting," becomes a kind of priest, a dispenser of sorely needed spiritual encouragement (otherwise known as grace) once you've decided to quit Maggie's farm.

And certainly it changes television. Without having any other entertainment—plays, movies, or even buying sprees—with much to modify, to soften the intensity of its effects, we found ourselves far more vulnerable to the glaring tube. News reports became grotesque distortions of reality. (Can that newscaster who's so stonily reporting the casualties of the latest invasion be *alive*?) *Laugh—In* was a threat to sanity, monstrously trivial. And the commercials, unfortunately, couldn't be tuned out as easily as newspaper ads. The pitch for sexy automobiles and "entire living room suites" for "only $199" began to nauseate me. How many people are being bombarded with pitches for things they never had and never will have: comfortable mattresses, sturdy kitchen utensils, refrigerators with zero-degree freezing compartments—or, slightly higher on the scale of solace for the urban-technological condition, air-conditioners, sound-deadening carpet-by-the-yard, humidifiers for little Johnnie's tender mucous membranes?

To my annoyance I still found these things seductive. It was as if deprivation, even though willed, served only to heighten their allure. To counteract this, I began reading selectively, voraciously, anything I thought would support me in my new way of life, whether it was *Rags* or the *Whole Earth Catalog*, Ivan Illich on free education or Robert Coles on the psychology of impoverishment. Slowly my ideas, once more theoretical than real, approached conviction.

There were changes that we hadn't, couldn't have, predicted. Ed's writing, for example.

Off and on, while working at regular jobs, Ed had written free-lance television pieces for *The New Republic*. He felt the magazine's political views were more or less consonant with his own, and after dropping out, he had thought to write more regularly for the magazine, but found, instead that the strain of putting things "their" way was becoming increasingly difficult. He wrote three pieces that summer before deciding that his views had become essentially different from theirs, and that he could no longer look to *The New Republic* as a market for his work. So our new life, with the altered perception of reality it engendered, had laid us a stymie. Not that *The New Republic* was any great source of income, but every $75 counts when you're not getting a salary.

In November, the opportunity to learn a new trade presented itself. A friend with a small construction business hired Ed as a full-time carpenter's helper. Having a weekly paycheck to count on rekindled our enthusiasm for the simple life. Small as it was (a base pay of $117 a week), we felt sure, again, that we could manage.

I still wasn't making any money myself. Having written what I prefer to think of as an investigation of cosmetic medicine but which I suspect the trade considers an exposé (would Jessica Mitford have countenanced the title *The Skin Game*?), I was now having to spend my time making the manuscript as libel-tight as possible. In past years I'd made $7,000 or $8,000 a year on free-lance magazine writing. In 1970, my total income came to a little under $3,000. But this book business couldn't go on forever. Could it?

In the beginning, Ed loved carpentry—work so purely, rhythmically physical that it left his mind free for contemplating the higher things, or so he kept insisting. He grew trim and brawny and permitted a full, rust-colored beard to flourish. His hands grew calloused and his nails split. He rose at six each morning in order to be down and across town for work by eight. Quitting time was 4:30, but he and the other guys were always trying to pack in a little extra time, so he rarely got home before 6:30. The sight of him night after night, plopped on the sofa in his thermal underwear, quart bottle of beer at hand, reading the paper or watching the tube, began to set my teeth on edge. I longed for the occasional dinner invitation so I'd get a chance to see how he looked in something other than the striped overalls he'd come to cherish as his second skin. Blue Collar is beautiful for a while, but did he really want to be a carpenter for the rest of his life?

These thoughts disturbed me, for who was I to impose my *Weltschmerz* on someone else? I also saw that if I, too, were making $117 a week, we wouldn't have a money problem and I really wouldn't give a damn whether Ed was scraping paint or writing haiku. Should I look for a job? I was dying to get out of the apartment, away from the almost daily phone calls from creditors, the broken rocking chair, the windows we could barely see out of, and all those other reminders that the wheels of *my* liberation, at least, were grinding rather rapidly to a halt.

I looked at the editorial want ads. Several were placed by *Moneysworth*, a newsletter of consumer information published by that ex-dealer in erotica, Ralph Ginzsburg. I sent him a letter, along with tearsheets of a few of my published articles. Within a week I received a reply from Mr. Ginzburg informing me, in imitation Teletype with characters half an inch high, "Dear Mrs. Dowling, you are a first-class writer."

I have to admit I wasn't cold to the compliment. But before the marathon tryout project he'd requested (a dozen ideas for feature stories and one full-length article), I wanted to know what sort of job I was trying out for. I telephoned Mr. Ginzburg but couldn't induce him to name a salary. I did find out that the newsletter, which consists of six or eight pages of solid copy culled from sources as various as the FDA and *The New England Journal of Medicine*, was entirely researched, written and edited by two people. The publisher was apparently prepared to ante up some kind of salary for a third writer, but did I really want to work under the pressure of what I had already envisioned as Ginzburg's editorial sweatshop on West Fortieth Street? I didn't.

So much for my job-hunting efforts. The experience cleared up one thing for me. *I* don't want to work on Maggie's farm, either.

On the other hand, there's that cavity visible on Rachel's front tooth to think about. None of the kids has been to the dentist in almost a year. We still owe a patient man $475 for a bout of dentistry Ed and Gabrielle underwent before Ed left CPB. While we place an emotional priority on this bill, because of the decency of the creditor and the fact that he's a small businessman, unfortunately his bill gets shoved aside in favor of Eastern Airlines, Irving Trust, Con Edison and Ma Bell, accounts we have to keep up with for obvious reasons. These are the guys with the corporate clout. No tickee, no telephone. And we'd been *that* route on several occasions last year.

I knew we weren't eligible for Medicaid, yet the kids were clearly in need of dental care and would need medical care at some point (we'd been lucky so far), neither of which we could afford to purchase from private dentists and doctors. One day I went around the corner to the Riverside Health Station on West 100th Street to talk to someone about the problem. It was a friendly place. The waiting room was filled with babies, young children and their mothers, laughing, crying, gossiping. The inner-city marketplace; the well in the center of the village. I was the only white person in the room. I sat there for two hours, awaiting my turn with the social worker in charge of intake interviews. Shortly before three I had to leave because the kids were due home from school. I told the registrar I'd be back the next morning, but I never went back. True, my coat was as frayed as anyone else's in the room, but it was frayed by choice. Even if I were to qualify for social service, how could I, with my BA, my presumably marketable skills, my experience, foist myself onto the overloaded schedules of clinic doctors who were treating patients without any options?

Options. That word was beginning to cause me increasing concern. Did I have the option to pursue my own craft, the kind of work for which I'd been educated, trained—*conditioned*, even— if by it I couldn't earn enough money to provide for the basic necessities? Did Ed have the right to opt for honest work, work that did not compromise his most profound beliefs and thus drive him close to insanity, work that, in short, made him feel good about himself, if by it he couldn't ensure the health of his children?

In the absence of any immediate resolution to that dilemma,
I decided to try the free-lance hustle from which I'd so far been
protected because of my dependence on Ed's income. You blanket the market with queries, pester editors on the phone, try out
your ideas relentlessly, not stopping when you've heard "No, it's
not quite right for us" a dozen times. Brazenness has never been
my style, but too bad. Buckwheat spaghetti five nights a week
has never been my style, either.

It's odd, although I guess in retrospect it's not really so star-
tling, but as soon as I arrived at this decision—not to rely on Ed's
taking care of me, not even to *want* Ed's taking care of me—my
whole view of myself fell out of its symbiotic lock-up with Ed.
One night, long after everyone else had gone to bed, I was sitting
in the bathtub and was struck by one of those pungent, life-
swerving insights that occur, I think, only several times in a lifetime. I saw how incredibly mushy I'd become. I no longer knew
which opinions were mine and which his. Was that *my* feeling
about the justice of Calley's sentence, or was it Ed's? Did I give
a damn about brown rice, or Claude Levi-Strauss, or thinking-in-
whole-systems? For how long had I been trying to sell myself Ed's
notion that to use paper toweling is to commit a reactionary act?
What did I really think of Dan Berrigan?

I know what I think of Dan Berrigan, with his "like, man's"
and his "I'm hip to's." I think he panders to a culture that's alien
to him, the street culture, as a matter of political expediency. I
think he's *not* being pastoral when he tells a young mother whose
husband has just gone off to jail instead of war, and who asks him
what jail is really like, "*Man*, jail is a beautiful experience." And
what about those pasty-faced nuns he hangs out with? Is that
courage they're demonstrating, or is that simply shooting up for a
revolutionary high?

I told these things to Ed and he flashed a recognition of all
the ways in which he, too, had been strangulating on The Marriage.
We figured that the only way we could stay together, if at all, was
to break the contractual bonds, including the sexual ones, and
hang loose. No program. No guarantees.

After a winter of staying home every night for want of baby-
sitter money, we got the bright idea of taking turns. He'd grab a
friend and go off to the West End bar for an evening of talk over
a couple of slow beers. I'd go down to the Village for dinner with
a friend, not worrying about the time, home on the 2 a.m. subway,
happy, reading the morning *Times*. I joined a Tuesday night singing
group and was pleased to find I could still sight-read difficult

music after thirteen years away from it. So we were seeing far less of one another and enjoying it more.

In March, word began to go around Ed's work crew that the brownstone they'd been renovating was almost finished and there were no more jobs lined up. The owner of the company told Ed he'd have to lay him off in a couple of weeks.

With this imminent lifting of what he now perceived as yet another yoke, Ed tasted the sweet salt of liberation once again. This time he'd find a part-time job so he'd be sure to have enough time to write. He had an idea for a book that would be fun to work on, and commercial as well.

Two days later, while sloshing a dozen house shutters in a vat of lye solution, Ed, thinking about his book, whistling, enjoying the cold and being outdoors, paddled the stuff too vehemently and got lye on his face and into his eye. It was his miraculous fortune that the one other man on the premises grabbed a bucket and filled it with water as soon as he heard Ed screaming out back. He poured the water on Ed's face and took him to the hospital. The doctors found it difficult to comprehend, but the eye appeared not to have been seriously damaged. It was an exciting injury, though. "You want to see a fresh lye burn?" they called to one another.

Ed came home early that afternoon with an enormous eye patch, abrasions on his cheekbones, burned lips and a seriously shaken soul.

Getting the paint off the shutters had been the last chore for Ed on this job. The boss wasn't too interested in sending Ed back on the lye and Ed wasn't too interested in it himself. Thus, his job was terminated sooner than we had counted on. We had Ed's final paycheck of $96 and nothing else. Since the first of the year, I had earned $1,000 which had gone for three months' rent and a tuition payment on our four-year-old's nursery school. (That's right. With all our other financial problems, we have a child in private school. It's a middle-income cooperative, one that I helped found, and for $21 a week Rachel is well cared for from nine to four each day while I work.)

Ed applied immediately for unemployment insurance and learned that he would receive $69 a week, but the process could take months. (It was five weeks before we received our first unemployment check from Albany.) In the meantime, what were we to do?

We were visited by an out-of-town friend who had once worked for the city's welfare department. "If I were you," she said, "I'd go right down and apply for family assistance. That's a sort of emergency thing. The way it looks to me, you're eligible."

Welfare. Public assistance. The dole! Had that dream of a year ago—Ed at his typewriter, I at mine, sunshine slanting into the study at noon, Bach in the morning and rock in the afternoon—been less idyllic than insane?

Before this moment, we had never conceived of the possibility of needing welfare. Ed came from a background that equated welfare with the Bowery. I had been brought up to believe that education is the best policy. Once the degree is in hand, you are insured for life against the possibility of need.

Ed strapped himself together and went down to Welfare the next day. I'm happy to report that they did not squint into his soul for signs of welfare chiseling. Certain facts, apparently, were in Ed's favor: a history of steady employment, military service, three kids and a wife who was still with him. But didn't he have any savings? "No. I was only making $3.50 an hour." God. Go down to the veterans' office. They can speed up the intake process. And don't feel bad about this. You owe it to yourself, and to your family. This is an emergency.

And it was. And we didn't feel bad about it. Somehow we felt we were being realistic for the first time in months. Freedom is another word for nothin' left to lose.

Well, where to end all this, for in truth it's a story without an end. So far we've had four relief checks, $57 each. Freddy, the manager of the Mom and Pop grocery around the corner, won't cash them. Says the city checks are the easiest paper of all to hang. Some welfare recipients cash them and then call in to say they never arrived in the mail. The caseworker stops the check. When Freddy calls the welfare department to ask why payment was stopped, the city tells him it's none of his business. Ed had six or seven appointments with an opthalmologist, compliments of Workmen's Compensation, before being assured that his eye was out of danger. In addition to his weekly visits to our local unemployment center, on 90th Street, he has paid a goodly number of required visits to the welfare department. As any welfare recipient can verify, proving eligibility can take almost as much time as a regular job.

But those four checks for family assistance have given us something more than food, I don't mind telling you. It's a relief to be on relief. Heads clear. Ideas come. Work progresses. Ed has been writing several hours a day and doing a lot of library research

for his book presentation. Oh, I know. By the lights of the welfare system, Ed should be making the 7 a.m. shape-ups and I should
be selling eyelashes at Macy's. But would that really be productive? Would that make any sense at all?

Me? It's ironic, but the month on welfare has given me the
peace of mind to sit back and recollect, to lay all of this out for
you. People have said to me, "If you write that piece for *New
York*, you'll blow the welfare gig." But that's the point. We
don't view welfare as a gig. We don't even view the city as Yaddo.
It's just the way things happened. We took a chance, we got into
trouble, and the city is temporarily bailing us out. Is that any
stranger than the idea that our parents worked in airplane factories
during the war, put us through college, deferred their pleasure until they were old in order to pass on to us The Great American
Dream, or any stranger than that, after years of working for The
Man, we upped and decided to take that dream as our reality?

IV

Forecasting
the Future of the Family:
Continuity
and Diversity

12

Prospects for Change in American Sexual Patterns

John H. Gagnon and William Simon

The authors of this selection take a position on the "sexual revolution" which is somewhat more thoughtful than that found in popular articles and also in the writings of other authorities. Gagnon and Simon argue that many of the changes in sexual behavior which have startled and upset some persons are neither recent phenomena, nor are they a revolution. The changes in sexual norms and practices are the consequence of a gradual release from earlier constraints controlling sexual behavior, especially that of women.

They point out that the sexual nature of man was brought out into the open by Freud and other early psychiatrists and the veil has now been removed from the discussion of sex. What was formerly studied in the privacy of the doctor's office has now been studied on a more collective basis, notably through the work of Kinsey and his associates.

This kind of analysis should make us more critical and less naive not only about present sexual practices but also about de-

John H. Gagnon and William Simon, "Prospects for Change in American Sexual Patterns." Reprinted from *VD—The Challenge to Man*. Published January, 1969, by American Social Health Association, New York, N.Y. Copyright: John H. Gagnon.

This paper was originally presented by Mr. Gagnon at the National Conference of the American Social Health Association, New York, October 27-28, 1968. Support for the research done for this paper came from Public Health Service Grants: HD 02257 and MH 14929.

scriptions of the past and predictions of the future. Just as historians evaluate carefully the accounts of man's past thoughts and behavior, so must sociologists scrutinize as critically the glib forecasts of the future.   —GFS

* * *

We live in a society that, if it is marked by nothing else, is, at least on the surface, undergoing nearly constant change.

   Yet this paper's title poses the issue as if little major change had taken place. This is in direct contrast to the points of view of many persons who would argue that the title ought to be "The Revolution in American Sexual Life." These persons would go on to say that most of the major changes in these patterns have already taken place. However, the evidence is that very little has changed in American sexual patterns over the past four decades, and if we are to understand the relationship between sexuality and the larger social order and the role that sexuality plays in the life of the individual, this fact must be confronted. This point of view provides an agenda through which one can begin to specify some of the problems that are involved.

   The first item on the agenda is the character of the evidence that suggests that up until this point in time and this current generation of young people most aspects of sexual behavior have not changed.

   The second item is the matter of why large numbers of reasonably well-informed persons would believe that things are changing when in fact the evidence suggests that they are not. One might note briefly that there are three sources to this belief in change, a belief that appears to be a form of systematic self-delusion. The first is the relatively recent capacity of persons in this society to engage in public talk about sex; the second relates to the ways in which we still talk about sex in our private worlds; and the third is the ideological struggle that has been going on about what the consequences of a revolution in sexual values might be.

   The third major item is a consideration of what nonsexual changes have taken place in the society and the relation of these to the constancy of sexual practice. A last concern is with the kinds of changes that can be legitimately expected to occur and the role that sex will have in the lives of young people who are growing up today.

Our first concern is to examine the existing evidence about sexual behavior to see if it supports the contention that a basic change in sexual practices has taken place in this society, and to assess what evidence there is which indicates the direction of such change. Before turning to the topic that has attracted the most concern and is at the root of most discussions of a sexual revolution—that is, premarital coitus among the young—it must be noted that the society's interest in sexuality is extremely uneven. Few are interested in the complex problem of an eroding sense of masculinity which results from a meaningless or an absent occupational life and the role intercourse plays in affirming masculinity. Even fewer are interested in the unwanted conceptions that result from sexual intercourse that is directed toward shoring up a sense of manhood. Even more directly related to sexual behavior, few are interested in the problem of masturbation and the role it plays during adolescence in the development of the male sense of identity.

SEXUALITY ROUTINELY DISCUSSED

The society has gotten to the point where it can now discuss sexual acts and entertain itself with discussions of who might be doing them; however, this interest tends to focus on the young or the deviant and hence is discussion which itself might be a substitutive form of sexual behavior. As a consequence of this skewed set of interests, nearly all discussions of changes in sexual values or behavior have focused on only three topics in addition to premarital coitus. These are: (1) orgasm on the part of the female; (2) extramarital coitus; and (3) homosexuality, especially on the part of the male. Much that follows in this discussion of premarital coitus applies to these topics as well, although there certainly are differences in the character and intensity of concern. Premarital coitus most pervasively occupies the center of attention because of the convergence of the topics of youth, sex and anxiety.

The kinds of specific changes that are popularly thought to be taking place in premarital coitus are:

1. Premarital coitus is occurring with a greater prevalence; that is, more young people are doing it.

2. Premarital coitus is occurring with greater frequency; that is, they are doing it more often.

3. Premarital coitus is occurring more promiscuously; that is, they are doing it with more different people.

4.   Premarital coitus is occurring under conditions of lowered affect; that is, people are doing it with people they do not love.

It is important to note that most of this moral concern is with
girls (perhaps read "daughters" here) rather than boys, since female
virginity still retains its tie to marriageability and property value.
This tie between the hymen (both actually and symbolically) and
the significance of the purely coital sexual experience has obscured
the meaning of the premarital sexual relationship, especially as it
occurs on the part of the female.

On the level of prevalence, it does not appear that there is any
body of research evidence leading to a belief that the figures generated by Kinsey et al. for the period 1925-1945 from an admittedly
limited sample have radically changed. Data recently gathered for
Mr. Vance Packard indicate there may be an increase in the proportion of college-going females who are not virgins. The ultimate
meaning of these figures, however, is still in doubt. The proportion of a population having coitus before marriage can only be calculated from a population that has completed the premarital period, that is, from interviews with those married. What Packard's
data do indicate is that for the college-educated the arena for premarital coitus has moved from the post-college to the college years.

However, there is no evidence that among those who are engaged in premarital coitus it is occurring with any greater frequency
than previously. The evidence that girls now have intercourse with
a larger number of males than in the past must also rest upon very
weak grounds. Given the declining average age at marriage, which
has somewhat stabilized recently, there is evidence that girls who
marry earlier have coitus with fewer men than those who marry later. This is surely to be expected, since there is no evidence that the
age at which first coitus occurs is declining, into the early teens, regardless of the age at marriage, and this narrowing age band results
in a smaller number of years of exposure to the possibility of coitus.

MIDDLE-CLASS PATTERNS PREVAIL

These same three factors may be examined with reference to males
as well. It is possible, logically speaking, that there are more conservative patterns of premarital coitus (that is, lowered incidence,
lowered frequencies, and greater affection) among males now than
there was in the past. With increasing significance and potency,
middle-class patterns of social life and courting have penetrated
the rest of society. It is therefore possible the previously discovered high rates of premarital coitus on the part of the lower-class

men may be declining toward the lower middle-class patterns. The middle-class pattern is one of restraint and deferral of gratification, and with increasing numbers of young people entering college from all social levels, the constraints of the middle class may actually be becoming more generally applied. The impact of the middle-class courting pattern may be leading in this direction as well. If middle- and lower-class patterns converge, it will be far closer to the style of the former than the latter.

The notion that premarital coitus is occurring under conditions of reduced affection misses the central nature of premarital sexuality in American society. Premarital coitus is surely disapproved, but the extent and intensity of disapproval decline with the closeness to the marital bond. It might even be called "normal" deviance, since it is seen as a part of the normal patterns of the courtship experience. While not approved as such, the stigma attached to premarital coitus is certainly not serious, if it is performed in the context of this courtship process.

What is observed is a continued development of a process which has continued for some 40 years in American society: the gradual release of the female from earlier constraints on premarital coitus and mate selection. With the increased anonymity and mobility of urban society, the mating process has become more and more one of exchanging increasing levels of sexual intimacy on the part of the female for increasing emotional commitments on the part of the male. The romantic ideology is still endemic, as is the image of sexuality as an experience which ought to be accompanied by overwhelming passion. Given these conditions and the above-mentioned potential for middle-class patterns to penetrate downwardly to at least the stable working classes, the continued intertwining of sexuality and emotion before marriage seems nearly inevitable.

BURDEN OF CONTRACEPTION UP TO MALE

It is precisely these conditions which control the nature of premarital coitus that make all of the current talk about the increased use of contraception on the part of the female seem so absurd. Until the female approaches a point near marriage, or until her relationship with a man is defined as being emotionally stable, with marriage as its goal (really here defined as proto-marriage), the burden of contraception will continue to fall into the hands of the more or less competent male, for it requires basic change in self-definition to create the female's capacity to plan and use contraception. It means that she is ready, or least prepared, to have coitus on a particular night. It does not suggest that she will be swept away by love or attraction, but that she will self-conciously admit a sexual concern and interest that may be alien to her. This is not a widespread capacity among most females before marriage, even though they are quick to assume the use of contraception after marriage, especially in the middle-class.

What events would be convincing evidence that a major change in premarital coital patterns had taken place? It would have to be the converse of the conditions of coitus noted above: that coitus among females now occurs with large numbers of males outside the context of marital preparation and that contraception is now deemed the responsibility of the female. The sheer increase of incidence of behavior or the particular increases and decreases of frequency would not be convincing evidence as long as these changes are in the service of getting married and starting a family. The revolution would occur when the context of values and meanings attached to acts changes, not when there are small-scale differences in rates or incidences. Such rate changes may well interact with value changes, but it is the social and psychological context that provides meaning for sexual expression and not the latter for the former.

If this argument is valid—that actual changes in behavior in this area are slight—what has provoked the imagery of change? Its sources may be located in three interrelated areas. The first is the relatively recent discovery of the shift in patterns of premarital coitus that occurred nearly 50 years ago, and which is still working out its consequences today. The belatedness of this discovery is a consequence of the fact that only recently has an attempt been made to examine sexual lives, not of individuals—since Freud began this long ago—but as a society and a collective entity. Most people are still in the process of locating themselves in a sexual arena that has a public dimension. This is part of the reason for the remarkable response at all levels to the two Kinsey volumes of about 15 and 20 years ago. The books were a means by which people were delivered from a private conception of sexuality to a public one. The shock and surprise were not the particular percentages or the tables, but rather the placing of words in public context that were previously meaningful only in private. The Kinsey volumes were an occasion for a collective confrontation with sex that had occurred for American intellectuals a generation before when they discovered Freud and psychoanalysis.

In a curious way, this event recapitulated in the life of society the way individuals in their own lives are surprised by the sexuality of others. Sexuality is learned in a context of secrecy, in small peer groups, or in the dyadic situations; and the intensity of the denial of sexual needs and experiences results in their repression and a low order of salience. When a sexual event does emerge in public view, it is as if it were *de novo*. Since a few people spend much time thinking about sexuality, at least in terms of its general meaning, any information concerning it comes as a surprise. It is not that no sexual change has occurred in the society; it simply happened as part of a general social adjustment between 1900 and 1920 that was not chronicled or noted until well after it happened.

HOW PEOPLE TALK ABOUT SEX

In addition to a new confrontation with sexuality, there is a second salient element which stems from the same situation of pluralistic ignorance about sex: the way in which people talk about sexuality in this society.

The following examples suggest the importance of language to the process by which talk has created an image of sexual revolution. This first example, however, arises in its general form from a situation that is removed from sexuality. If someone gets up in the morning with the flu and exhibits sufficient symptoms of distress such that others notice the fact, then in any conversation that occurs during the rest of the day he is queried about his condition if he chooses to have a stiff upper lip, or he tells others about it if he chooses to seek social support. One of the rules of social interaction states that when our man says something about his case of the flu, the person he is speaking with also has to say something about the flu. He reports that he too has had it, his children now have it, that someone he knows died from it, etc. The man who is ill is therefore a target for all flu stories (including remedies for treatment and sympathy) in the immediate environment. It is perfectly possible that he might then say over the dinner table, "there sure is a lot of flu going around," when in fact the rate of flu infection is no higher than it usually is, and indeed may possibly be lower than usual. Our hero is thus a self-perceived repository of a flu epidemic, an epidemic that has been created by the rules of talk.

In the sexual area, there is little direct evidence about actual behavior, and where behavior that does occur is in private, there is very little observational or even systematically reported information that can serve as a check on the sexual talk flowing through a community at any one time. It must also be realized that sexual talk is produced for a variety of reasons and that, given the entanglement of sexuality with guilt and shame, the motivations that exist for the talk are diverse and complex. Most of the talk is surely situation specific, for, as Bell and Buerkle have shown, mothers do not approve of premarital coitus for their own daughters, while daughters may well do so, even though there is little evidence that the rates of such coitus have changed from one generation to the next. From Ehrmann and others there is supporting evidence that girls before marriage are more likely to approve of premarital coitus, whether or not they have such coitus, if they are in love or are engaged. The impact of these changing life situations and the experience with sexuality, as well as other kinds of experiences, surely structure the character and direction of sexual talk.

HOW FORECASTS FOR FUTURE ARE MADE

This structure of private talk could not produce the revolutionary mythology if it did not get caught up in the two ideological postures with reference to sex that exist in the society today. These postures may be best characterized as the sexual yeasayers and the sexual naysayers. They are the ones who convert the private fantasies and the private talk of the society into collective myths and opposing ideologies. They both make forecasts of the future, the yeasayers focusing on a glorious sexual revolution that will release human energy to produce a utopian social fulfillment. The naysayers forecast social and moral collapse and point to the pseudo-parallel of Rome.

There is an air of confidence about these kinds of forecasts which is naively facile, and they are at most indirectly relevant to sexuality and to its complex interrelations with personality, social structure, or systems of values. Further, what is even more suspect about the confidence shown in these predictions is that they are based on little besides the desires, feelings, and impressions of the predictors.

However, these two groups who have the strongest opinions about sex are also the most vocal, agreeing on the fact of revolution even though disagreeing on its consequences. The naysayers are those for whom any sexual change is seen as the beginning of an inexorable decline in the moral condition of the society. Opposing them are the yeasayers who feel that if sexual problems could only be straightened out, then everyone would be able to live a happy, healthy productive life; that sexual freedom will somehow decrease racial tensions, improve the lot of the poor, educate the illiterate, and put an end to the causes of war.

Both of these groups suffer from the same delusion (as perhaps do we all): that sexuality is a primary moving force in human experience and, if it were only regulated either by suppression on one hand or by total freedom on the other, the problems that face mankind would be resolved. This is surely a delusion, especially the view of the naysayers, for their propositions have long since been shown to be absurd; however, there is as little evidence to support the positions of those who would save us through sexuality; it is by its very nature a dependent variable. It is something that is more caused than causing, and only through its ties with other human experiences is it given its meaning. The act of sexual intercourse may be an act of love or an act of aggression or both simultaneously. The act of masturbation may be purely a reduction of physical tension, an act brought about by the absence of a desired sexual object, or an act of extreme complexity, involving both of the forementioned purposes and others, and having important symbolic overtones for the actor. None of these meanings can be derived from the act itself nor can the act itself produce such meaning.

Our knowledge and ability to deal with sex are obscured by its ideological use on the public level where it provides the metaphors of either societal or individual decay or corruption, or societal or individual resurrection. On the individual level we are caught up in private ignorance about sexuality, misjudging its meaning to ourselves and others and rarely knowing what motives we are acting out or in service of what needs we are doing sexual things. As a consequence our conversations about sex at the societal level rip it out of context and confer on it powers that it does not have and effects that it cannot create.

WHY HAVEN'T SEXUAL PRACTICES CHANGED?

The third item on the agenda becomes salient at this point—why have not our sexual practices changed? After all, nearly everything else in the society has changed. The litany of technological, scientific, economic and social changes in the society is nearly endless. The society seems to be moving into an era dominated by the megalopolis, super-cities that can extend from Boston to Washington, San Francisco to Los Angeles. An era has opened in which automation, complex organizations and the institutionalization of innovation and invention will become a national way of life. Many elements have been part of this vast remaking of the face of America, a remaking fundamentally unplanned and unthought out. How many in 1946 would have planned the massive social dislocations that the suburbs, the automobile, the superhighway, the TV set and all of the other apparatus of American life have left in their wake? Planned or not, desired or not, these are the opening moments of the post-industrial society, a society which, regardless of the state of its poor and disfranchised, has as its first generation one which has grown up without a major depression, truly children of affluence.

Part of all this change has been events that everyone thought must surely lead to vast changes in sexual behavior. The move to the suburbs gave the children earlier dating, allowing them to model themselves on the manners and styles of their affluent elders. Barby and Ken dolls became teenage models for the fantasies of little girls. There is a 15-billion-dollar-a-year teenage market. The automobile has become endemic, and young people spend more time out of the house and in the peer group than ever before. There is the fallout from the medical revolution—a revolution that doubles medical knowledge every five years—penicillin to cure VD and the pill to prevent pregnancy. In the cinema there are displays of nudity and books have become more openly sexual. At the same time more young people are going to college—millions of them newly away from parental supervision. And one should not discount the young men in South East Asia living in a new culture with new values. Each of these events has been greeted as the moment of sexual downfall (or utopia): the car, the pill, rock and roll music, each in its turn has been greeted with almost prurient pleasure by those who are addicted to the sexual apocalypse.

SEX SUFFERS FROM OVERKILL

Why did it not work? As one looks around, most young people, even those who protest, are busily going about the business of mate selection that will eventuate in marriage and children. Among the vast silent, but not necessarily happy, middle class that still dominates the landscape of American youth, getting married and getting a job and a house are still their central concerns. What else was really expected to happen? What was expected was that young people, when the constraints on freedom of all sorts were released, would do what adults thought they might do (but also would not have): go out and have a sexual ball. The problem is that sex is not a beast lurking ready to lunge out and run amok if but one chain is removed from it. Sex has really been suffering from societal overkill.

In the midst of all this change young people have been taught pretty much what previous generations were taught about sex. That boys are usually sexier than girls. That masturbation was something that one didn't do or one kept it a secret if one did. That there were good girls and bad girls and you married one and not the other. And everyone busily made sure that the girls knew all about the cosmetic aspects of sex—remember Barby and Ken have no genitals, only wardrobes—but nothing about sexual pleasure. And every day society said that sex was part of getting married and falling in love. And most young people, even those who do have premarital intercourse, believe what they are told.

The most important message of all of this is that sex is quite frankly only a marginal kind of drive. It does not turn off and on because it needs to express itself. It, like everything else, needs to be learned. Sex is only realized and sexual arousal only occurs in social situations which are designed to elicit sexual responses. The evidence for the case of successful management of this ostensibly powerful drive is the comfort with which lives of celibacy are lived by many men and women both in and out of the clergy.

The reason that there was not any change was that many of the things that were thought to have something to do with sex didn't have anything to do with it. Further, there were already so many constraints that removing just a few barriers without providing an environment in which someone could develop a new set of reasons for the behavior provided nothing. What this means is that without creating a learning situation in which sex could be given a new connection to other aspects of social life there is no good reason to expect any change.

WHAT WILL HAPPEN NEXT?

If there has been no change, and if the society has suffered from a delusion about the power of sex, and if most of the things that were thought to have had something to do with sex don't, what will happen next? These are only guesses, but one might estimate that the drift of the society will be to a situation where sex will diminish in its importance in terms of being either a source of major guilt or a source of major salvation. There seems to be settling on the land a cooler tone in many aspects of interpersonal relations. Part of this is a result of automation and organization. There is no man's work except in very small pockets of the society. The old skills that promoted a sense of durable manliness—hunting, fishing, hard physical work that it was presumed that women could not do—have turned into leisure time sports, a relief from the management of paperwork and people. Working up a sweat now only occurs at play, not at work. The skills that the Boy Scouts teach are now relevant only to the leisure time of the adult and not to the realities of apartment house and Levittown existence. In all of this the role of women has changed very little, and today they are even more committed to the home and children than they were in the 1930's during the last gasp of feminism. Thus the male role moves closer to that of the female, not in terms of increasing the number of homosexuals, but in moving toward the management of people rather than things. Out of this one might expect somewhat of a revolution in terms of declining significance of sex on the part of males and an even greater linkage of sexual activity with affection and attachment.

The burden of masculinity will be more and more linked to style, dress, cosmetics and the like. At the same time there will be a softening of the edge between women's and men's roles which can be seen in the hair length and clothing of young people today. Even the hypermasculine clothing is merely a cosmetic gesture to affirm for certain periods transient role differences. Perhaps the basic changes in sexual styles will come after marriage and during the periods between marriage as the total proportion of broken marriages in the society tends to increase.

Most of life will still be lived in the family; however, there may be more families per individual lifetime, but the sexual motif is likely to decline in significance. Sex will move out of the center of stage as a source of passion and return as a form of play—as a parallel to gourmet cooking. There will be no Romeos and Juliets because no one will be able to develop a level of passion sufficient to die for either love or sex. This is the likely outcome of a modern society, not the sudden release of sexual passion, but sexuality played out in a new key, less important, less central, less overdetermined. Neither as corruption nor salvation.

13

Facts and Forecasts
about the Family
and Old Age

Gordon F. Streib

The latter part of the family cycle has not been studied with the
same interest and depth as earlier phases of the cycle. This is due
to the fact that later life has negative implications in Western societies, particularly the United States, which is very youth oriented.
However, the facts of life and death show that many persons will
live as many years after retirement as they do from birth to marriage. Hence from the standpoint of years alone, there is need to
carefully consider what family patterns will be like for the middle aged and the old in the decades ahead.

   Will there be more isolation of older persons from the young?
Will more older persons start a second marriage late in life? Will
their children be the major opponents or will they permit parents
the same freedom they demand for themselves? Is the "empty
nest" a trauma for parents? These are a few of the questions
raised in this selection.

   In all three of the articles in this section, the authors engage
in the hazardous undertaking of forecasting the future. This task
is undoubtedly very difficult, given our limited knowledge of the
present from which the extrapolations are made and the instability
of a changing dynamic society.   —GFS

From *American Behavioral Scientist*, Vol. 14, Number 1 (Sept./Oct. 1970),
pp. 25-39, by permission of the publisher, Sage Publications, Inc.

There has been an increasing interest among scholars, scientists, and journalists in what life will be like in the year 2000 (Winthrop, 1968). It is surprising how little attention is given in this growing literature to family structures and relations, especially those of the latter part of the life cycle.

Why has the older family been ignored? First because the study of old age is not as popular and interesting as predictions of technological advances. It is concerned with decline, deceleration, and death, and thus tends to be avoided or ignored. In our youth-oriented culture, old age is not considered a captivating topic to study.

Some of the older utopian societies, such as the Shakers or the Oneida community, were concerned with the roles of older people (Nordhoff, 1875; Carden, 1969). However, in the descriptions of new forms of family relationships which one reads so often these days in the popular press, the entire emphasis is placed on the family relationships of young people. There is no mention of the problem of "Grandma in the commune."

Finally, the family is regarded as a dependent social form which is influenced by technological and economic factors; thus it can respond to change but cannot stimulate or influence it.[1]

The major information base which will be drawn upon for our discussion and analysis will be the United States. We assume, however, that many if not most of our observations, particularly the facts and the forecasts which we make, would apply to other Western industrialized countries. The primary reason for assuming the basic similarity of family structures and relations in Western industrialized societies is the fact that the detailed, careful, cross-national study of Denmark, Great Britain, and the United States by Shanas et al. (1968) has shown strikingly similar findings for these three societies.

It should be stressed that the forecasting of family structures and relations for a generation ahead is not a scientifically well-grounded operation (Goode, 1968). The fragmentary body of knowledge which we possess is based upon limited samples of information gathered with the use of crude instruments. Moreover, the theories of social change pertaining to the family—as well as to other social institutions—are rudimentary, and this is particularly true about the future of industrialized societies.[2]

FORECASTS FOR THE FAMILY IN OLD AGE

In this section we will outline some of the major facts and trends concerning the family and old age, and on the basis of this knowledge, we will forecast the characteristics of family life and family structures pertaining to later maturity in the year 2000. For the sake of clarity we have assigned these trends to three broad categories: (1) Biosocial, (2) Sociocultural, and (3) Social-Psychological. There is obviously some degree of overlap in these categories, but they can be regarded as constituting three distinct analytical levels.

Biosocial

These characteristics are rooted primarily in biological phenomena. Social and Cultural factors impinge upon them, and social scientists consider them usually as demographic factors or variables.

1. The life expectation for white males is approximately 68 years and for white females about 75 years (Riley et al., 1968: 28-29). We forecast that the length of life will not be greatly extended for most persons (Kahn and Wiener, 1967: 51-57). Major scientific discoveries may well be made in the biological and medical sciences which will alter this possibility. However, some investigators seem to be rather conservative in their expectations about major scientific breakthroughs regarding major causes of death for older persons such as heart disease, cancer, and stroke. Medical gimmickry, involving such things as heart transplants, may contribute to our knowledge of human anatomy and physiology, but major organ transplants will not be widely practiced and, therefore, will not affect the longevity of very many older persons.

2. Women live longer than men. The life expectancy of men and women has increased over a long period of years, but since the turn of this century, the differential in the expectation of life between the sexes has steadily increased (Riley et al., 1968: 28-29). The universal fact that throughout the animal kingdom, the female of the species is longer-lived appears to be a persistent biosocial trend. The continuation of this trend implies that the present tendency for many more women than men to become widowed should be a stubborn fact of family life for at least a generation and probably longer.

Sociocultural

These facts and trends are more closely linked to social and cultural components of society than those listed under Biosocial. They are more closely related to the norms, attitudes, and values shared and transmitted by most members of the society.

1. About nine out of ten persons eventually marry. The trend for more adults to marry at least once will continue to be a major cultural pattern.

2. Men marry women who are on the average three or more years younger than themselves. The tendency of men in most cultures, and specifically in the United States, to choose younger women for marital partners will not change. This culturally influenced pattern will continue to accentuate the larger proportion of widows than widowers in the older population.

3. We anticipate that the increasing concern with environmental problems—many of which are highly correlated with population pressures—will result in smaller families. More families will have one, two, or no children than in the present older generation. The smaller family will result in fewer grandchildren.

Social-Psychological

These trends can be conveniently classified under three kinds of family role relationships: husband-wife, parent-child, and sibling.

Husband-Wife Relations

1. The basic family unit in old age is the marital dyad, for among persons 65 and older, 53% are married couples (Riley et al., 1968: 159). A broad picture of all persons over age 65 in the United States shows that 71% live in families with other persons to whom they are related and 22% live alone (Riley et al., 1968: 167). Only about 12% of older married couples live with their children (Riley et al., 1968: 168). "Intimacy at a distance" will continue to be preferred by both old and young as the living arrangement for older persons. Unless there is a radical decline in the standard of living—which might necessitate some doubling up in housing—married older couples will prefer to live separately from their children.

2. American society has more permissive sexual norms than a generation ago. The forecast for the next generation is that there will be an increased understanding of the fact that sexual activity is normal in older persons. The fuller understanding of man's sexuality and the greater permissiveness in which the present generation has been reared will result in more tolerance of older persons having platonic and sexual liaisons than is common at the present time.

3. Mid-life divorce is on the increase in American society. This trend will continue into the next century. Marriages may be continued for the sake of children, but when children reach maturity, there will be a greater proneness to terminate a marriage. Greater numbers of divorces among the old will probably be associated

with more remarriage. There will also be more remarriage of widowed persons (McKain, 1969: 123). The remarriage of older persons will have repercussions for parent-child relations (McKain, 1969: 108-122) because of the problems related to the transfer and disposition of property, visiting patterns, and family assistance patterns.

Parent-Child Relationships

1. Contrary to some of the stereotypes about the rejected old person, there is considerable contact between old parents and their adult children. Even though the residential family may consist of only one person, the modified extended family remains an important part of the older person's life.

In the study of three industrialized societies (Shanas et al., 1968: 174) it was reported that most older parents (over three-fifths) had seen at least one child the same day of the interview or the previous day, and another fifth had seen a child within the previous week. The percentage of older persons who had not seen a married child in the previous year was very small (three percent). This existence of an extended kin network in which parents and children are in regular and frequent contact with one another will continue and may increase in the decades ahead. The assertion by some theorists that the isolated nuclear family is the modal pattern in American society is not supported by a variety of studies in the contemporary situation, and isolation will not characterize modal family patterns in the future.

2. Reciprocity patterns are evidenced; adult children and their parents maintain a viable kin network involving mutual patterns of assistance. Small services are rendered reciprocally by each generation. In the United States more than half the older persons reported they helped their children (Shanas et al., 1968: 204-205). Moreover, the aged are independent of regular monetary aid from their children. In the United States, only four percent report receiving regular financial aid.

The reciprocity of help—shopping, housework, baby-sitting, home repairs, and so on—as a form of kin assistance will continue as a family pattern into the next century. The overwhelming percentage of the old now report receiving no regular financial aid from children. This pattern will persist, unless there is a major economic depression, a catastrophe, or a major social restructuring.

3. The postparental period is not a traumatic and negative experience for most families, in spite of gloomy reports of the "emp-

ty nest" syndrome (Deutscher, 1964: 52-59; Gurin et al., 1960: 92-93, 103). A number of cultural trends will tend to perpetuate this pattern in American older families. The fact that more women will be employed outside the home suggests that their lives will have other foci than child rearing. Furthermore, the increasing emphasis on the dangers of overpopulation and the desirability of small families, coupled with the pronouncements from women's liberation groups that women have a destiny other than as breeding machines, will encourage women to have broader interests. Opportunities for travel and other leisure pursuits also suggest that parents will be able to find substitute interests for family-centered activities. With the problems of the "generation gap" and the increasing cost of higher education for children, many families will find the "empty nest" period a time of contentment and fulfillment.

Sibling Relationships

Living with siblings will not be an important form of living arrangement except for the single—never married—person. Even the widowed or divorced do not live with siblings. This pattern will continue into the generation ahead.

SOCIETAL TRENDS

The following trends are more remote from the family itself, but they will have profound effects upon family structures and relations. These trends are an integral part of the larger trends in post-industrial American society.

1. Most older persons will live in their own homes, but there will be more specialized communities and residences which will be age segregated (Walkley et al., 1966).

2. The average age for retirement of men is about 65. There are an increasing number of retirement plans which permit an early retirement option. The retirement age will decline in the years ahead as a result, in part, of economic benefits received by a person when he elects to retire early. The probable consequences of more persons retiring early will be that a larger proportion of older persons will change their residence for climatic reasons, kinship consideration, (to be near children or other kinsmen) or to have a smaller and more comfortable home. However, the large majority of retirees will continue to live in their long-term place of residence.

3. There will be improved health and medical care provisions which will release the immediate family from some of the health care costs which it assumed in the past.

4. Assuming no major restructuring of the economic and political systems, there will be improved pension and social security benefits. More persons will be able to retire earlier on special early retirement plans. Despite these gains and also assuming some moderate growth in the economy, the aged in general will continue to be an economically underprivileged segment of the society.

QUALIFICATIONS AND VARIATIONS
FROM THE MAJOR PATTERNS

These generalizations must, of course, be qualified for subgroups and subcategories of the population. The importance of major variables which have been found to influence social relations and human behavior in the past may be changed to some degree in the next generation. But it seems probable on an intuitive basis, projecting past trends into the future, that ethnic, religious, racial, residential, occupational, and educational factors and variables will be significant in qualifying, modifying, or accentuating most of the above generalizations. We believe that the struggle for racial, religious, and social justice will continue and will probably accelerate in the decades ahead. Moreover, there will be definite positive changes in the social, economic, and political situation of the underprivileged and those groups and categories of the population which suffer discrimination.

The major ethnic and racial minorities—Blacks, Mexican-Americans, and the American Indians—will receive more opportunities than in the past, yet a pragmatic forecast suggests that substantial numbers of these minorities will continue to be underprivileged compared to the majority of white Americans. The most difficult and unresolved internal social problem will be the situation of Black Americans. The matri-focal family continues to be a significant pattern among lower-class Blacks (Frazier, 1939:Billingsley, 1968) and it is forecast that increased social insurance benefits will alleviate somewhat the stringent economic situation of the lower-income Black family in their gerontological phase.

Among lower-income and less-educated white Americans, one can also expect that socioeconomic differences will continue to be observed concerning the latter period of life. For example,

Kerckhoff (1964) found that professional and managerial couples welcome retirement and have a more favorable experience in retirement while lower occupational levels tend to be more passive in advance of retirement and they report their retirement experience more negatively.

RADICAL RESTRUCTURING OF THE SOCIETY
AND THE FAMILY

Social scientists do not have a very high batting average in predicting the broad course of human affairs, and it is probably risky to make prognostications about these matters. However, with all of the hazards that such activity entails, we propose the following possibilities.

We believe that there is a low probability of radical restructuring of American society. The general institutional structures will continue to be organized in about the same way—government, the economy, education, and so on. There will be modifications, of course, but it is unlikely that in the next decade or two the capitalistic economic system with government intervention in some sectors will be changed in its major contours.

How will this affect the family? Even if there should be a major restructuring of the society—for example, governmental ownership and control of major industries, banks, utilities, and the like—the family as an institution and as an interacting group will tend to operate basically in the ways which are familiar to contemporary Americans, with emotional and mutual help patterns of prime importance. We note that in other countries having undergone drastic change—Communist China and the Soviet Union—family structures, because of their resiliency and tenacity, are not quickly altered. There may be some adaptations to meet the exigencies of possible inefficiences which might result from the drastic alteration of the political and economic systems, but the family members will continue to interact as a primary group.

If a radical restructuring of the society does occur in the next generation, the likelihood of the present middle-age cohort faring better under the restructured society is not great. First, the radical restructuring is more likely to be initiated and carried out by young people and if successful, younger persons would tend to be the power wielders in the new system, such as has occurred in Cuba. Second, assuming even the most orderly radicalization and smoothest transition, there are likely to be periods of strain and areas of neglect. Even if the reorganization should be carried out with a minimum amount of force and violence, the old are likely at best to find themselves in a state of "benign neglect" unless the new regime can maintain a high level of productivity equal to that of the old order. The care and treatment of the old is rather highly correlated with the general level of economic development and social security of the society as a whole. Hence, it is unlikely that the aged will receive any special consideration.

In this connection, it is interesting to observe the situation of the aged in Russia since the time of the complete restructuring of that society with the goal of more humane treatment of all Soviet citizens. One of America's leading students of the Soviet family reported in 1968 that a half century after the Bolshevik revolution, only about half of the Soviet population is covered by social security (Geiger, 1968: 204). Coverage is provided only to those who have worked for an extended period. Geiger also reported that only 38% of the women over the legal retirement age of 55 were receiving pensions in 1959. The Soviet family has adapted to the lack of adequate pensions for the aged and the shortage of homes for the aged by the use of a three-generation extended family form. Geiger (1968: 205) summarized the situation in these words:

> In the marketplace of mutually desired services it has been a good bargain; in exchange for a home, the aged have taken over, according to capacity, the functions left undone by the working wife and mother. In past years this arrangement has been such a standard practice that it was defined as desirable. In the words of a worker: "It is good when both spouses work and have someone to do the laundry and cooking, etc." All benefit from this arrangement, including the Soviet regime itself, which saved itself the expense for many years of becoming a true welfare state.

NEW FAMILY STRUCTURES ON A MICRO-SCALE

We have asserted that there is a low probability there will be a major alteration of the political and economic structure of the United States in the next generation. Further, if a major restructuring should occur, its immediate chief effect upon many older families will be a decline in the standard of living.

There is another way in which *some* American families might be changed in their basic structure and relationships and that is by the creation of collectivities, enclaves, cultural islands, and settlements which would foster or develop family forms which would differ from the modal pattern found in the larger society. The number of persons who might live in collectivities would probably be relatively small in proportion to the total population, but their influence might be greater than their sheer numbers might suggest.

Historically, the United States has been the haven for the settlement of peoples from abroad who desired to pursue a way of life which might be variant from that of their neighbors. The United States has also spawned a variety of indigenous groupings with norms and values which differ from those of the larger society. Some of these ethnic, religious, or cultural enclaves survive, while others have been short-lived. Among those from abroad which have maintained their cultural identity for a long period have been pietistic groups like the Amish who have lived in the United States for over two centuries (Hostetler, 1968).

Broadly speaking, these American communities can be dichotomized into those which were (or are) organized on the basis of private property or those in which property is collectively held—communal societies. The study of these communities indicates that those in which property is held privately by individuals or by blood relatives are longer-lived than those which have the communal ownership of property.

In this connection, it is pertinent to study the communes of Israel. The kibbutzim have had to confront and cope with the problem of an aging and aged population. To my knowledge, the communes now being organized in this country have given no attention to gerontological issues. This is, of course, quite understandable because their major concerns are ideological, membership recruitment, internal tensions, and sheer survival in many cases. However, if any remain viable long enough, at the turn of the century, they will face similar problems to those which the kibbutzim of Israel have encountered. One of the interesting facts found in the perceptive report by Talmon (1961) is that Israeli communes have a form of benign disengagement in which persons disengage gradually, and probably with less strain than may be true of older persons in the larger Israeli and American society. However, what is more significant from the standpoint of the family in old age is that parents of the members who move into the kibbutzim in later life are happier and more contented than the aging members who have lived in the commune for long periods, for the latter are often very critical. Moreover, the parents of the members, as new residents, do not have the ideological commitment to youth, work, and productivity, and are not pressured by group norms and behavior as are the older members. They are grateful to be there and do not suffer the decline in status and power which the older members must face. The aging member who has had an integral position in the settlement and adheres to its values must face more pressure and strains.

There is a marked increase in retirement communities in the United States (Walkley et al., 1966), and it is instructive to compare them in terms of structure and ideology with the communal settlements of Israel and of this country. This comparison offers valuable clues about some family and community issues in the decades ahead. The retirement village or retirement home usually requires the payment of a substantial fee for the purchase of an apartment or house, or for lifetime lodging. The terms, conditions, and housing may vary considerably but our concerns here are not real estate and economics but family structures and relations. The person who moves into a retirement community buys his house or apartment as an individual private investment and pays for it and the community facilities which are involved. It is primarily an individual economic decision and occurs because the person or his family can pay the cost involved. There are few, if any political or ideological aspects involved. On the contrary, young people who join communes (this was and is true of the Israeli kibbutzim) have strong and deep ideological reasons in almost all cases. Idealism is high and the economic considerations are rather low in the priorities. It must be pointed out that while ideological motives can be very powerful, they have a certain fragility and instability and are subject to alteration due to shifts in beliefs and also because of the economic and social pressures which arise internally and in the larger society. Hence, in the long run the ideologically organized commune faces a different set of problems from those of the retirement community which is established primarily for economic reasons.

It is predicted that retirement villages, based on economic considerations combined with community interest, will continue to flourish in the United States. However, they will remain a middle-class phenomenon and will not involve any real sharing of resources, but will continue as contractual arrangements based on the ability of the person or his family to buy this style of life.

CONCLUSIONS

In the future old families will find that they are increasingly in competition with other groups in the society, such as militant youthful, racial, or ethnic minorities who will be seeking a larger share of the community's funds. There will continue to be a struggle for federal and local funds and resources. Unless the old become more militant, which is doubtful, they will never get as much concern and attention in American society as they would like. Furthermore, there are three inescapable problems over which they have little or no control: inflation, declining health, and for the women, widowhood.

Yet there are many optimistic aspects to the forecast of life ahead for the family in old age. With increasing social security benefits, improved medical insurance, and more widespread pension plans, more older families can look forward to declining years of comfort and fulfillment. If they are adaptive, they will be able to maintain their own residences, as they overwhelmingly prefer, and still remain in close emotional contact with their kin networks.

NOTES AND REFERENCES

1. William J. Goode (1963: 18) is one sociologist who has stressed that the family may be an independent factor influencing the process of industrialization. William F. Ogburn in his early work stressed the impact of technology upon other institutions. In Ogburn's (see Ogburn and Nimkoff, 1955) later work, his approach was much more intricate for he analyzed technology linked in complex ways to other causes of changes in the family. The statement of Fred Cottrell (1960: 92) would probably be accepted by many as a summary of the issue: "There is probably nothing on which social scientists agree more completely than upon the thesis that, to a very great extent, social change is tied up with technological change."

2. Goode (1968) has offered an excellent analysis of both the major theoretical questions concerning social change and the family and also the kinds of data required to obtain some tentative answers.

Bell, D. (1967) "Introduction," pp. xxi-xxviii in H. Kahn and A. J. Wiener (eds.) The Year 2000. New York: Macmillan.

Billingsley, A. (1968) Black Families in White America. Englewood Cliffs, N. J.: Prentice-Hall.

Carden, M. L. (1969) Oneida: Utopian Community to Modern Corporation. Baltimore: Johns Hopkins Univ. Press.

Cottrell, W. F. (1960) "The technological and societal basis of aging," pp. 92-119 in C. Tibbitts (ed.) Handbook of Social Gerontology. Chicago: Univ. of Chicago Press.

Deutscher, I. (1964) "The quality of post parental life: definitions of the situation." J. of Marriage & the Family 26 (February): 52-59

Frazier, E. F. (1939) The Negro Family in the United States. Chicago: Univ. of Chicago Press.

Geiger, H. K. (1968) The Family in Soviet Russia. Cambridge: Harvard Univ. Press.

Goode, W. J. (1968) "The theory and measurement of family change," pp. 295-348 in E. B. Sheldon and W. E. Moore (eds.) Indicators of Social Change. New York: Russell Sage Foundation.

———(1963) World Revolution and Family Patterns. New York: Free Press.

Gurin, G. et al. (1960) Americans View Their Mental Health. New York: Basic Books.

Hostetler, J. A. (1968) Amish Society. Baltimore: Johns Hopkins Univ. Press.

Kahn, H. and A. J. Wiener (1967) The Year 2000. New York: Macmillan.

Kerckhoff, A. C. (1964) "Husband-Wife expectations and reactions to retirement." J. of Gerontology 19 (October): 510-516.

McKain, W. C. (1969) Retirement Marriage. Storrs, Conn.: Storrs Agricultural Experiment Station.

Nordhoff, C. (1875) The Communist Societies of the United States. New York: Schocken Books.

Ogburn, W. F. and M. F. Nimkoff (1955) Technology and the Changing Family. Boston: Houghton-Mifflin.

Riley, M. W. et al. (1968) Aging and Society. New York: Russell Sage Foundation.

Shanas, E. et al. (1968) Old People in Three Industrial Societies. London: Routledge & Kegan Paul.

Talmon, Y. (1961) "Aging in Israel, a planned society." Amer. J. of Sociology 67 (November): 284-295.

Walkley, R. P. et al. (1966) Retirement Housing in California. Berkeley: Diablo Press.

Winthrop, H. (1968) "The sociologist and the study of the future." Amer. Sociologist 3 (May): 136-145.

14

North American Marriage: 1990

Leo Davids

In the last selection, Leo Davids extrapolates from our present knowledge to predict what marriage and the family may be like in the next generation. His forecast of things to come is based upon a realistic assessment of the present-day situation, taking account of changing trends in child rearing, mate selection, and family relations which he thinks will be more widely and ultimately institutionalized as part of our society.

    Predicting that romantic love will some day be considered "quaint," Davids thinks that more rational criteria for marriage will be adopted. —GFS

* * *

As a preamble for this attempt to predict the options and regulations defining marriage and family life in North America a generation from now, let us consider some of the powerful long-term trends in this area which can be discerned either at work already,

Reprinted with permission from *The Futurist*, published by the World Future Society, Post Office Box 19285, Twentieth Street Station, Washington D. C. 20036.

or coming very soon. These provide the casual principles that will be extrapolated here to provide a scientific indication of what the mating and parenthood situation is going to look like in another two decades. The remainder of the paper is essentially a working-out of this prediction exercise so that an account of the new situation is built up, which is the best way we have to predict the nature of marriage in 1990.

"PARENTHOOD IS FUN" MYTH WILL DIE

1. The foundation of almost everything else that is occurring in the sphere of marriage and family life today is a process which will go right ahead in the next decade or two, and will continue to have a vast effect on people's thinking and their behavior. This process is what Max Weber called the *entzäuberung*, the "demystification" or "disenchantment" of human life, which is a hallmark of the modern orientation. Young people, especially, are continually becoming more sophisticated—due to television, modern education, peergroup frankness about all spheres of life, etc.—and they are no longer accepting the myths, the conventional folklore, upon which ordinary social interaction has been based during the past few decades. Thus, for instance, young people are gradually rejecting the myth of "parenthood is fun," realizing that parenthood is a very serious business and one which ought to be undertaken only when people are ready to plunge in and do a good job.

Another grand complex of myths that is gradually being rejected is that of romantic love, under which it is perfectly accceptable to meet a person, form a sudden emotional attachment to that person without any logic or contemplation, and to marry that person on no other basis than the existence of this cathexis. Similarly, the whole institution of "shot-gun weddings," in which an unwanted, unintended pregnancy (usually occurring with a lower class girl) leads to what is called "necessary" marriage, is going to become a quaint piece of history which will be considered with the same glee that modern readers feel when they read about "bundling" in Colonial America. With young men and women who are all fully-informed about reproduction and what can be done to prevent it, such things will occur very rarely; romantic mate-selection, likewise, is going to continue only among the impoverished and marginally-educated segment of society.

Insofar as family life remains almost the only area of modern behavior that has not yet become rational and calculated but is approached with unexamined, time-honored myths, we can expect that this area is "ripe" for fundamental change. When serious, critical examination of all this really gets moving, very great changes will come about in quite a short time.

PROCREATION CAN BE SUBJECT TO COMMUNAL CONTROL

2. The second independent variable leading to the developments that we are discussing is the total control of human fertility which advances in medical technique have made possible. There is no need here to discuss the pill, intra-uterine device (IUD), and the many other ways that are in use already to separate sex from reproduction, and therefore to free relations between men and women from the fear or risk of begetting children who would be a by-product, an unintended side-effect of fulfilling quite other needs. This control of human fertility means that what procreation does occur in the future is going to be by choice, not by accident. Both illegitimacy and venereal disease will be almost extinct, too, in 20 years. It also means that reproduction and child rearing can henceforth be subjected to communal control, will be potentially regulable by society at large. Without contraception, all the rest of these trends and changes would not be occurring at all.

HUSBAND-WIFE EQUALIZATION IS "INEVITABLE"

3. Women's Liberation, I believe, is not a fad or a current mass hysteria but is here to stay. Once the schools had instituted co-education, male dominance was doomed. Let us rephrase that term for present purposes, calling it Husband-Wife Equalization, as a general name for certain tendencies that have been evident for many years and are continuing today. We all know that marriage has shifted, to borrow a phrase, from institution to companionship. Indeed, through the demystification-sophistication of young women, their employment in full-status work, and because of the control over reproduction that has now become a reality, the equalization (in regard to decision-making) of wives with their husbands has become inevitable. The implications of this are already being voiced, to some extent, in the platforms and proposals of women's rights organizations, and some points will be touched upon herein.

It must be remembered that there will remain in the foreseeable future, a traditionalist minority even in the most advanced and change-prone societies. This segment will expend much effort

to maintain patterns of marriage and family living that they feel
are right, and which are consistent with the patterns they experienced when they were children. This traditionalist minority will
certainly not be gone, or vanished to insignificant numbers, in the
short span of one generation; therefore, any predictions we make
must take into account not only what the "new wave" pattern is
going to be, but also the fact that there will be a considerable
number of people who elect to maintain the familiar value system
that they were socialized with, and to which they are deeply com-
mited.

LAW WILL ACCEPT ABORTION AND
NEW FORMS OF MARRIAGE

4. Another trend which is already at work and which, we may
assume, is going to accelerate in the future is that legislatures no
longer attempt to shape or create family behavior by statute, but
are, and increasingly will be, prepared to adapt the law to actual
practice, so that it accepts the general viewpoint that public opinion has consensus on. I think that ever since Prohibition, legislators have been forced to agree that sooner or later legal reform
must narrow the gap between law on the books and what is really
happening in society. It is likely that this reforming and correla-
tion is going to be speeded up in the next few decades, so that
the extent to which there is an uncomfortable and problematic
contradiction between the law in force and what people are really
doing will be virtually eliminated. Thus, all of the ongoing changes
with regard to contraception, abortion, new types of marriage
contract, etc., will—it is here assumed—be accepted and in a sense
ratified by the Law, as the old-style moralists who can still be
found in our agencies of social control cease to fight a rear-guard
action against the new norms that are, whether they like them
or not, emerging. All modes of birth control will become medical
problems, free of any statutory limitation.
5. An important consequence of widespread social-science knowledge among young people today, which is coupled with a greater
use of principles drawn from sociology and anthropology in the
process of law reform, will be the recognition that continuity or
consistency for each person or married couple is necessary, in
regard to the larger questions at least, for a particular marriage
system to work well in the long run. If the agreements entered
into, whatever their content, involve major inconsistency, if people

seem to be changing the fundamental norms between them in midstream or giving much more than they receive, then obviously the community has unwisely allowed these people to enter a situation which must lead to disorganization and conflict sooner or later. This realization from our functionalist understanding of how marriage—or any continuing relationship—operates, will lead to acceptance of the clear necessity for such predictability and fairness in every particular case.

So much for the preamble. What are the consequences? Two major principles underlying our model of marriage in 1990 emerge from the forces and trends listed above. They are: (a) the freedom to personally and explicitly contract the type of marriage one wishes; and (b) formal public or communal control over parenthood.

What is meant by the word "marriage," here? To include the newer forms, we require a looser, broader definition than would suffice in the 1950s. Marriage should therefore be understood to refer to a publicly-registered, lasting commitment to a particular person, which generally includes certain sexual or other rights and obligations between these people (that would not be recognized by their community without such married status).

Free choice of the sort of marriage one wishes does not mean that a man and woman (or two men or two women?) will write their own original contract incorporating any combination of rules and arrangements that they like. The reason that such freedom would be beyond that envisioned in our thinking, as argued above, is that they would be able to invent a contract that has severe internal inconsistencies or flights of self-delusion, and which therefore sets up strains for their relationship from the outset. The sophistication which anthropological functionalism has brought to us will lead society to channel the choice of marriage into a selection from among a number of recognized types, each of which has been carefully thought through so that it is tenable in the long run. Thus, people will select from among various ways of being married, each of which makes sense by itself and will enable them to function on a long-run basis once they have had this choice. Neither monogamy nor indefinite permanence are important in this respect, so they will not be required. However, the agreed-upon choice will be explicit and recorded so there's no question of deception or misunderstanding, as well as to provide statistical information, and official registration of this choice is an element of marriage which will remain a matter of public concern.

PEOPLE UNFIT TO BE PARENTS WILL BE SCREENED OUT

The right of society to control parenthood is something that can be predicted from a number of things we already know. For one thing, the rising incidence of battered and neglected children, and our almost total inability to really cope with the battered child's problem except after the fact, will certainly lead legislators to planning how those people who can be discovered, in advance, to be unfit for parenthood may be screened out and prevented from begetting offspring who will be the wretched target of their parents' emotional inadequacies. Furthermore, increasing awareness of the early-childhood roots of serious crime and delinquency will also lead to an attempt to prevent major deviance by seeing to it that early socialization occurs under favorable circumstances. It does not appear that there will be many other really effective ways in which rising crime rates could eventually be reversed. This, however, will again mean that those who raise children will have to be evaluated for this purpose in some way, so that only those parents who are likely to do a respectable job of early socialization will be licensed to release new members of society into the open community. If such testing and selection is not done, we have no way to protect ourselves from large numbers of young people who have been raised in a way that almost inevitably will have them providing the murderers, rapists and robbers of the next generation. Since we now begin to have the technology and the knowledge to prevent this, we may confidently expect that parent-licensing is going to come into force soon.

One other trend, perhaps phrased from the negative side, must also be mentioned here as we try to describe the norms that will probably circumscribe marriage in another generation. This trend is the decline of informal, personal social control over married couples which was formerly exercised by kinsmen and neighbours. It would not make sense to anticipate massive changes in the law and explicit contractual entry into marriage as the normal way to shape married life, if mate selection and the interactions between husband and wife were still under the regulation of custom, vigilantly enforced by aunts, grandfathers or brothers-in-law. It is precisely because the vast mobility of modern living has led, along with other factors, to the isolation of the nuclear family—which is the source of so many problems in the family sphere today—that this new kind of regulation will be called into force and accepted as necessary and proper. The recognition that marriage has left the sphere of *Gemeinschaft* will help to bring about a consensus that the regulation of this area of life will have to be handled like any other kind of socially-important interpersonal behavior in today's *Gesellschaft* civilization.

COURTSHIP MAY BE "DUTCH TREAT"

What will courtship be like in about twenty years? We can assume that courtship will, as it does currently, serve as a testing ground for the kind of marriage that people have in their minds, perhaps even dimly or unconsciously. Thus, insofar as particular young men or women may have begun to feel that the type of marriage they would like is Type A rather than Type B, their courtship would be of the sort that normally leads to Type A, and in a sense tests their readiness to build their relationship along those lines. Only the traditionalist couples will keep up such classic patriarchal customs as the male holding doors, assisting with a coat, or paying for both meals when a couple dines out together. The egalitarians would go "Dutch treat," i.e., each paying for himself, during this spouse research period. Thus, courtship will be of several kinds corresponding to the kinds of marriage that we are about to describe, with the conventional acts and phases in the courtship signalling the present intention of the parties involved to head toward that kind of marriage. Thus, pre-marriage and marriage will exhibit a psycho-social continuity, the early marriage centering on the basic interpersonal stance that is already represented in courtship.

Of course, courtship will serve this testing and assessing function after people have been approximately matched through computer mate-finding methods. Random dating and hopeless courtships will have been largely prevented through the provision of basic categoric information which people can use to screen possible spouses, such as total years of schooling completed, aptitude and IQ scores, major subjects (which are related to intellectual interests in a very direct way), religiosity, leisure and recreation preferences, and similar things.

For remarriage suitors, data on wealth or credit and occupation would also be used, along with some indication of attitudes concerning home life and procreation. Since homogamy (similarity between spouses) is recognized as an important indicator of marital success, such information will be systematically gathered and made available to cut down on the wasteful chance element in mate selection. It is only when people are continuing their search for a spouse within the appropriate "pool," defined in terms of those who are at the right point with regard to these variables, that courtship as a series of informal but direct experiments in relationship-building will come into play.

CELIBACY WILL BE LEGITIMIZED

Explicit choice of the kind of marriage one enters into is, of course, an effect not only of the emancipation of women but of men as well. What will some of the major options be? With the insurance functions that were formerly secured by having children (who would provide during one's old age) being completely taken over by the government (assisted by unions, pension funds and the like), there will be little reason to warn those who choose childlessness against this course. With celibacy no bar to sexual satisfaction, society will accept the idea that some segments of the population can obtain whatever intimate satisfactions they require in a series of casual, short-term "affairs" (as we call them today), and will never enter any publicly-registered marriage. With celibacy or spinsterhood fully legitimized, and with no fear of destitution when one has retired from the labor force, there will undoubtedly be a sizeable number of people who decide not to enter into a marriage of any sort on any terms.

TRIAL MARRIAGE FOR THREE OR FIVE YEARS

Another not-unfamiliar option in this regard will be the renewable trial marriage, in which people explicitly contract for a childless union which is to be comprehensively evaluated after three years or five years, at which point either a completely new decision can be reached or the same arrangement can be renewed for another term of three or five years. This would not be, then, a question of divorce; it is simply a matter of a definite arrangement having expired. The contract having been for a limited term, both parties are perfectly free to decide not to renew it when that term is over. This would be a normal, perhaps minor, part of one's "marital career."

A third option, which introduces very few complications, is the permanent childless marriage; the arrangement between the two adults is of indefinite duration, but they have agreed in advance that there will be no offspring, and of course, there is no question but that medical technology will make it possible for them to live up to that part of the arrangement. Some will choose sterilization, others will use contraceptive methods which can be abandoned if one changes his mind and is authorized to procreate.

Compound marriages will also be allowed, whether they be polygamous, polyandrous or group marriages. However, these communes will not be free of the same obligations that any marriage entails, such as formally registering the terms of the agreement among the members; any significant change in the arrangements among members of such a familial commune will have to be recorded in the appropriate public place in the same way as marriages and divorces which involve only one husband and one wife. There will be great freedom with regard to the number of people in the commune, but internal consistency concerning the give-and-take among the members, their privileges and obligations, will be required. The functional, pragmatic ethics emerging in today's youth culture will be strictly adhered to, some years hence, not as moral absolutes, not because people have come to the belief that these represent the true right and wrong, but in order to prevent serious conflict.

LESS THAN THIRD OF MARRIAGES WILL PRODUCE CHILDREN

With the majority of young people in society choosing one of the foregoing patterns, the number of marriages in which children are expected will be relatively small; perhaps 25% to 30% of the population will be so serious about having children that they will be prepared to undergo the rigorous training and careful evaluation that will be necessary for them to obtain the requisite licenses. The marriages intended to produce children will usually be classic familistic marriages, in which the general pattern of interaction between husband and wife, as well as the relationship between parent and child, may be fairly similar to the contemporary upper middle-class marriage that we know in 1970. However, three-generation households will probably increase. I see no reason to believe that all of child rearing will be done in a collective way, as in an Israeli kibbutz or in the communes which have been set up in some Communist countries; infant care may gravitate in the direction of day nurseries, however, while school children will live at home, as now.

WOULD-BE PARENTS WILL HAVE TO PROVE THEIR SUITABILITY

The familial pattern, then, explicitly chosen by some men and women to perpetuate the classic familistic marriage, will be intended to provide a home atmosphere approximately similar to that which can be found in those middle class families of today's society that have the best socio-emotional climate. The community will be assured that this home atmosphere is, in fact, most probable, since it has been prepared for, rather than left to an accident of kind fate and to happenstance talents that people bring to parenthood nowadays. All those who desire to become parents, and therefore to exercise a public responsibility in an extremely important and sensitive area of personal functioning, will have to prove that they are indeed the right people to serve as society's agents of socialization. Just as those who wish to adopt a child, nowadays, are subjected to intensive interviewing which aims at discovering the healthiness of the relationship between husband and wife and of the motivation for parenthood, the suitability that the man or woman displays for coping with the stresses of parenthood, as well as the physical and material conditions that the adopted child will be enjoying, the evaluation of mother and father applicants in future will be done by a team of professionals who have to reach the judgement that this particular individual or couple have the background to become professionals themselves: that is, recognized and certified parents.

PARENT-TRAINING WILL BE INTENSE

The course of study for parenthood will include such subjects as: human reproduction and gestation; infant care; developmental physiology and psychology; theories of socialization; and educational psychology. Starting with a foundation of systematic but abstract scientific knowledge, the practical and applied courses in hygienic, nutritional, emotional and perceptual-aesthetic care of children will follow, in the same way as training for medicine and other professions. In addition to the subject matter referred to above, prospective parents will be required to achieve some clarity concerning values and philosophy of life, in which they will be guided by humanistic scholars, and will also be required to attain a clear understanding of the mass media, their impact on children, and how to manage mass media consumption as an important part of socialization in the modern urban environment. One side effect of such parent training may be a sharp drop in the power of the peer group, as parents do more and with greater self-confidence.

Suitable examinations will be devised, and only those who achieve adequate grades in these areas will be given a parenthood license. Some young men and women are likely to take the parenthood curriculum "just in case"; that is, although they have not yet thought through the type of marriage that they desire or the kind of spouse they are looking for, they may continue their education by entering parenthood studies and obtaining the diploma, should it turn out that they elect a classic, child-rearing marriage later on. Possibly, fathers will be prohibited from full-time employment outside the home while they have pre-school children, or if their children have extra needs shown by poor conduct or other symptoms of psychic distress.

One of the more striking areas of change, which can serve as an indicator of how different things will be then from what they are now, is age. Age of marriage now is in the early 20's, and child bearing typically occurs when women are in their middle twenties. Also, husbands today are usually about three to four years older than their wives. In another generation, the age of child bearing will probably be considerably advanced, as people who have decided upon parenthood will either be enjoying themselves during an extended childless period before they undertake the burdens and responsibilities of child rearing, or completing the course of study for certification to undertake parenthood. It is probable that women will bear children when they are in their middle and late thirties, so that they will have enjoyed a decade or a decade and a half of companionate marriage in which there was full opportunity to travel, to read, or just to relax before they have to spend 24 hours a day caring for a small child. As to the age difference between husbands and wives, which is essentially based on the patriarchal tradition that the man is the "senior" in the home, it will probably disappear in the case of all forms of marriage other than the classic familistic one; there, where people have explicitly decided that the kind of marriage they want is the same as their parents had back in the medievaloid 1970s, or the ancient 1960s, the husband will continue to be a few years older than his wife.

This picture of the marriage situation in 1990 leaves open various questions and problems, which should be touched upon briefly in conclusion. One of the difficulties in this scenario is the question of what authority will make the necessary decisions: What sorts of committees will be in charge of devising the various internally-consistent kinds of marriage, working out the parent education courses, and, certifying people for parenthood? There are, after all, political implications to controlling marriage and parenthood in this way, and the general public will have to be satisfied that those who exercise authority in this area are, in fact, competent as well as impartial.

Another problem is that of securing complete and valid information: (a) for those who are preparing to locate suitable mates through computer matching, or who are preparing to make a commitment in some specific form of marriage; and (b) concerning those who apply for the parenthood course and later for the license to practice parenthood. Unless we can be sure that the inputs used for making such judgements contain information which is adequate in quantity and true as well, these new systems will not be able to function without a great deal of deviance, and might easily engender problems which are worse than those which we confront today.

WILL CHILDLESSNESS LEAD TO
LESS LONG-RANGE INVESTMENT?

A third issue is that of parenthood having tied people to the community, and given them a commitment to the environment: What will childlessness do to one's motivation for planning/preserving; will it de-motivate all long-range investment? Research on this could start now, comparing parents with the childless.

Finally, we have assumed that marriage is going to continue, in some way. That is based on the belief that people will continue to desire a secure partnership with another person or small group, and that youth will feel it is better to institutionally buttress their sharing of life, in general, by setting up a marriage of some kind. This depends, in fact, on the interpersonal climate in communities, and the extent to which people feel isolation and unmet needs that marriage will solve. When marriage is not desired, then we will have discovered new forms of warm, dependable primary association replacing the old institution which has supplied psychological support to people through the millennia.

Suggestions
for Further Reading

I. Examination of the Issues

Adams, Bert N., "The Family in a Differentiated Society: Toward a Theoretical Perspective," p. 79-101 in THE AMERICAN FAMILY. Chicago: Markham, 1971.

Bernard, Jessie, WOMEN AND THE PUBLIC INTEREST. Chicago: Aldine-Atherton, 1971.

Cuber, John, "Alternative Models from the Perspective of Sociology," p. 11-23 in THE FAMILY IN SEARCH OF A FUTURE edited by Herbert A. Otto. New York: Appleton-Century-Crofts, 1970.

Goode, William J., "Introduction," p. 3-53 in THE CONTEMPORARY AMERICAN FAMILY edited by William J. Goode. Chicago: Quadrangle Books, 1971.

Laing, Ronald D., THE POLITICS OF THE FAMILY. New York: Pantheon, 1971.

Newson, John, and Elizabeth Newson, "Changes in Concepts of Parenthood," p. 139-151 in THE FAMILY AND ITS FUTURE edited by Katherine Elliott. London: J. & A. Churchill, 1970.

Rossi, Alice, "Transition to Parenthood," JOURNAL OF MARRIAGE AND THE FAMILY, 1968. *30*: 26-39.

Tavuchis, Nicholas, "The Analysis of Family Roles," p. 13-21 in THE FAMILY AND ITS FUTURE edited by Katherine Elliott. London: J. & A. Churchill, 1970.

II. Diversity by Fate and Choice in Marriage and Family

Komarovsky, Mirra, BLUE COLLAR MARRIAGE. New York: Random House, 1962.

Scanzoni, John H., THE BLACK FAMILY IN MODERN SOCI-ETY. Rockleigh, N. J.: Allyn and Bacon, 1971.

Shostak, A. B. and W. Gomberg (editors), BLUE COLLAR WORLD. Englewood Cliffs N. J.: Prentice-Hall, 1964.

Willie, Charles V. (editor), THE FAMILY LIFE OF BLACK PEO-PLE. Columbus, Ohio: Charles E. Merrill, 1970,

III. Case Studies of Diversity and Adaptation

Bartell, Gilbert D., GROUP SEX. New York: Peter Wyden. Reprinted in paper by New American Library, 1971. Signet Y4794.

Carden, M. L. ONEIDA: UTOPIAN COMMUNITY TO MODERN CORPORATION. Baltimore: Johns Hopkins University Press, 1969.

Geiger, H. Kent, THE FAMILY IN SOVIET RUSSIA. Cambridge: Harvard University Press, 1968.

Hedgepeth, William, THE ALTERNATIVE: COMMUNAL LIFE IN AMERICA. New York: Macmillan, 1970.

Hostetler, John A., AMISH SOCIETY. Baltimore, Md. Johns Hopkins University Press, 1968.

Hostetler, John A. and Gertrude Enders Huntington, THE HUT-TERITES IN NORTH AMERICA. New York: Holt, Rinehart and Winston, 1967.

Houriet, Robert, "Life and Death of a Commune Called Oz. NEW YORK TIMES MAGAZINE, February 16, 1969. Reprinted in THE CONTEMPORARY AMERICAN FAMILY edited by William J. Goode. Chicago: Quadrangle Books, 1971, pp. 276-290.

Lopata, Helena, OCCUPATION: HOUSEWIFE. New York: Oxford University Press, 1971.

McKain, Walter C., "A New Look at Older Marriages, "THE FAMILY COORDINATOR, 1972, 21: 61-69.

Moskin, J. Robert, "The New Contraceptive Society," LOOK, February 4, 1969, pp. 50-53. Reprinted as "Sweden: The Contraceptive Society," in FAMILY IN TRANSITION edited by Arlene S. Skolnick and Jerome H. Skolnick. Boston: Little Brown, 1971, pp. 187-193.

Nordhoff, C., THE COMMUNISTIC SOCIETIES OF THE UNITED STATES. New York: Schocken Books, 1965 (originally published 1875).

Young, Kimball, ISN'T ONE WIFE ENOUGH? New York: Henry Holt, 1954.

IV. Forecasting the Future of the Family: Continuity and Diversity

Adams, Bert N., "The Family in the United States: Retrospect and Prospect," p. 348-360 in THE AMERICAN FAMILY by Bert N. Adams. Chicago: Markham, 1971.

Christensen, Harold T. and Christina F. Gregg, "Changing Sex Norms in America and Scandinavia," JOURNAL OF MARRIAGE AND THE FAMILY, 1970, 32: 616-617.

Edwards, John N., "The Future of the Family Revisited," JOURNAL OF MARRIAGE AND THE FAMILY. 1967, 29: 505-511.

Toffler, Alvin, "The Fractured Family," Chapter 11, pp. 238-259 in FUTURE SHOCK. New York: Random House, 1970. Reprinted in paper by Bantam Books, 1970.